ACTING
On Your Faith

CONGREGATIONS
Making a Difference

ACTING
On Your Faith

CONGREGATIONS
Making a Difference

A Guide to Success in
Service and Social Action

Victor N. Claman and David E. Butler
with Jessica A. Boyatt

A Making a Difference Book

INSIGHTS
Boston

This book is printed entirely on recyled paper. Printed in The United States of America

9 8 7 6 5 4 3 2 1   **ISBN 0-9639701-0-0**

TO ORDER ADDITIONAL COPIES
or to sponsor free distribution
please see inside the back cover
or call 1-800-323-6809

*Dedicated to you and your congregation
and the enormous potential for making
the world a better place.*

For everything there is a season,
and a time for every purpose
under heaven.
Ecclesiastes

PREFACE

On the way to the office

This is a book that's been more than two years in the making. It was written for you — laypeople and clergy struggling with how your congregation can best "put your faith into action." Soon it will go to the printer and then find its way into your hands.

Today is a beautiful August Monday, and it's the day to write the introduction, something which most writers leave to the very end. Just an hour ago I was walking to my Boston office, and despite the fine weather — or perhaps because of it — I was fretting about being able to write something that would "grab" you.

Although there are homeless people on the streets here, as there are in most cities in this country, this morning there were none in sight. As I walked the last two blocks, thinking how hard it would be to find the right words, I noticed a battered car with a family in it. Even in the quick glimpse I got as I walked by and the car moved slowly past me in the opposite direction, I could see this was no family on an August vacation.

In the right front seat was the mother, a worn-out woman perhaps in her mid-30's, looking late 40's. Behind her a teenage girl looked at me with dark apprehensive eyes and an expression bordering on hopelessness.

So...here on this beautiful morning, rolling down the streets of proper Boston, was this stark reminder that all is not well in God's world. The effect on me was startling — and welcome. I walked the next block with my eyes focused on the pavement, absorbing the fact that God's grace had stepped in to make my morning's work possible. There, right in front of me, was more evidence that there are people with deep problems, in desperate need of a way out of them. If we keep our eyes and hearts open, we will find them — and, as the people in this book have done, we will also find ways to enable many of them to get past their very real, everyday problems.

That's the central idea and purpose of the book: to help you find ways for your congregation to "make a difference" in people's lives. As you read the successes others have had, I'm sure you will see wonderful possibilities for your congregation to follow in their footsteps or to blaze new paths.

How the book happened

I think the story of how this book came into being will interest you. It illustrates my firm belief that life is a mystery and, while we can choose directions and even make specific moves, we can't always tell what twists and turns things may take.

I also think we must work with where we are, who we are, and what we have, and, as in the parable of the talents, we have to put our skills and assets to work and try to disregard the risks. That last part is hard.

I'm a layman, active in my congregation, a father of three grown children, a writer and publisher of consumer guides on energy conservation and other subjects, a person with sophisticated computers in the office and the ability to envision a publication and the persistence to make it become a reality.

Rather than delay the project by pursuing outside backing for the considerable costs for research and production, I decided to go ahead and begin the work, advancing my own financial resources. Sometimes, as the costs in both time and dollars were mounting, I thought, "This is out of hand! Why did I ever start this?" Even so, I continued, doing what I felt was needed to make the book effective. I was following a vision of what it could be and what it could accomplish: help stimulate a great deal of outreach and create a feeling of oneness across lines of faith and denomination, a feeling that we all are neighbors and can love one another, respect one another, understand one another, and do loving things. That we can all *be* love.

I've taken a risk on something I believe in. I think that's what we all must do. If we all fashion visions of how things might be and if we act on those visions, drawing on whatever resources we have, we *can* make the world a better place.

Partners in the struggle

Doing the book has been a real struggle for me, both to find the time and to deal with its complexity. Without two major occurrences it would have taken even longer and not come nearly as close to what I hoped it might be.

The idea for the book occurred to me a number of years ago, some time after I had been serving on my congregation's outreach committee. I tried to do the research while continuing with my other work, but it soon became apparent that it was a vast topic. I was turning up a fair number of stories, but that was clearly only the tip of the iceberg and there were many gaps. So I put the book aside with the intention of getting back to doing it after several other projects were out of the way.

One day in May, 1991, I got a call from a good friend, David Butler, a minister with a deep interest in outreach, who "just happened" to have some time available to consult on a good project. Over lunch, we discussed his possible involvement in "that outreach book" — didn't I agree it might be a good idea to get it off the back burner? From that conversation came more than a year's hard work on David's part as consultant, co-shaper, relentless pursuer of stories, drafter of write-ups, and visitor/photographer/interviewer at more than 40 congregations. Prodded on by my "Can't you find another West Coast church doing something wonderful?", David was key in making sure the book had national coverage, including multi-denominational and interfaith stories.

The second occurrence was when it came time to start the design and layout work. I had always thought this would be a picture book and hoped to find a person who shared my belief in the power of photos.

Jessica Boyatt, the person I chose as designer and photo editor, turned out to have skills I hadn't at all expected. She's a first rate professional photographer and a fine editor, able to cut where I couldn't, and had a major hand in shaping the *Possibilities* section. Many of the very best photographs in the book are hers. In her heart and mind she sees the wonder of human beings and has a very deep belief that things can and should be different in this world.

A transforming experience

As for myself, doing this book has been a transforming experience — turning what I *hoped* might be true into real life experience and confirming with my own eyes, ears, mind and heart that it *is* true. Having visited, interviewed and photographed at nearly 50 congregations in different parts of the country and read about hundreds more, having talked with David about his experiences, I now know it's possible for congregations to make a difference in a great variety of ways, and I know that doing outreach can bring a congregation to life.

It's also clear to me that Jews and Christians of every stripe have a great deal in common in their desire — and their actions — to make a difference. As you will see, a number of the stories are about churches and synagogues working together or of individual Catholic, Protestant and Jewish congregations in vastly separated places each doing the very same thing.

Finally, I know that through direct contact and "hands-on" projects, a oneness develops, a deep conviction that we are all part of one human race, that we are all God's people, all in the same boat, all living in God's world together, inextricably intertwined in each others' lives, fates and well-being.

All in God's good time — which is now.

So, the book has finally come together, "all in God's good time," as the expression goes. That time is now, not just for the book but for you too, as you and your congregation decide how you will reach out to make a difference. Whatever you choose to do, I firmly believe it will not only be helpful to other people, it will also be a transforming experience in your individual lives and the life of your congregation.

Victor N. Claman
Boston, August 16, 1993

IN APPRECIATION

Shown here are just a few of the faces that so warmly welcomed us in nearly 100 congregations around the country.

As we prepared this book, we came into contact with perhaps 1,000 people: clergy, denominational and ecumenical staff, and lay people in the congregations and their programs.

They showed and explained things to us, offered us their thoughts, referred us to others, supplied photos, fed us wonderful food, took us to their committee meetings and their worship services. All were enthusiastic and encouraged us mightily in our work.

We thank them all for their help, their hospitality, and their insights. This book is literally built on their contributions.

CONTENTS

Making a Difference

**An idea
whose time has come**

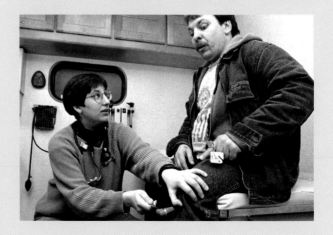

There's nothing so powerful as an
idea whose time has come.

Victor Hugo

AN IDEA WHOSE TIME HAS COME

Whatever your congregation calls it — "outreach," "mission," "social concerns" or "social action" — the focus is the same: "making a difference." Making a difference means enabling people to live fully in our world, to have and enjoy their fair share, to realize their potential and make their own contributions to a just and loving society.

Meeting Real Needs with Real Solutions

On a practical level, making a difference means working with people to help them meet real needs with real solutions. The number of people with needs, and the severity of some of those needs, have been escalating: today in the United States we have record numbers of illiterate people, many neighborhoods in decline, growing numbers of homeless people. Other kinds of needs — for a little help after school, for companionship, for caring — are also on the increase and call for attention. And, as we all know, people in other parts of the world face these and even greater problems.

A Unique Time

With all these needs around us, we're fortunate to be living at a unique time in history. It's a time of two things coming together: the approach of the year 2000 both challenges and empowers us to fashion new visions of what the world can be, while the tremendous resources at our disposal — time, talent, treasure, and technology — mean that many of those visions can become realities. It's also a time of choosing, a time to decide if we will commit those resources to make a difference in our world, if we will say "Yes! Making a Difference is an idea whose time has come!"

A Unique Resource

There's one more resource we have that is the key to whether we will choose to make a difference. It's our spiritual resource. One of its essential components is compassion, and we have an abundance of that. As one minister exclaimed when he heard this book was being written, "I'm extremely excited, because I know there's a vast reservoir of compassion, just waiting to be tapped!"

"Com-passion" — from the Latin, meaning "to suffer with" — is that quality of empathy that puts us in another's shoes. For deep inside we recognize ourselves in "them," and "they" cease to be "others" but rather, with us, part of the one great family of God. Something in us "connects" with their reality, with their efforts to make something better of their lives.

But clearly compassion is not enough, as Reverend Crilley recognizes so well (see p. 27 for story). We must actually do things.

Doing Things is Central To Our Faith

Whether we are Christian or Jewish, doing things that will make the world a better place for everyone is central to our faith.

The ethical imperatives are clear: wherever we look in the Bible, quotes abound: "Love thy neighbor as thyself." "Do justice, love mercy." "Love one another." "Set the captives free."

They are active words, and they call for action on our part. As it says in 1 John: "Let us not live in word or in tongue, but in deed and in truth." To use the Hebrew phrase from the Talmud, "Tikun Olam," we are admonished to "heal the world."

Why Your Congregation?

Nonprofits and government agencies do some of the same things that this book talks about: sheltering the homeless, feeding the hungry, building homes and redeveloping neighborhoods. Many nonprofits recruit volunteers and raise funds for their efforts; your congregation may even be one of their supporters.

With government and nonprofits involved, it's not unreasonable to ask why your congregation should be "in this business."

First, the biblical imperatives are numerous and clear, and you respond to them with a shared, explicit faith. While governments and nonprofits have believing individuals, your congregation's shared faith is a powerful spiritual resource: it motivates you at

"I know there's a vast reservoir of compassion out there, just waiting to be tapped."
Reverend Bob Crilley,
Fort Street Presbyterian
Church, Detroit, Michigan.

the beginning and enables and sustains you along the way.

Second, the needs are greater than the resources of nonprofits and often beyond the mood or mandate of government.

Third, outreach is a natural for your congregation. Yours is a real, continuing community. You meet regularly and are used to doing things. Your people have time, talent and treasure, energy and enthusiasm. You understand planning, organizing and fundraising. You may have an endowment.

You understand your home community and probably your metropolitan area. You know how things work, who the key people are and where to find needed resources. Your congregation commands respect and has access to press coverage. You have physical facilities and may be right in the center of things.

Finally, there's the vision of wholeness that you and your congregation have. All religious people have the same vision — of a society of justice and opportunity; of a community embracing a single race, the human race; of a world where "love thy neighbor" is the guiding principle for everyone. Because of your vision of wholeness you may just do outreach better — with greater care and imagination, with sustaining power, and with love.

An important but different reason to do outreach is that it can revitalize a congregation and make it grow — not just in numbers but also in depth of understanding and richness of spirit. When you work with others to help them solve their problems, you learn from them, you have opportunities to grow and change, you find that living out your faith increases your faith as individuals and as entire faith communities. So, through your outreach, as you give you are also receiving gifts from those you work with, and from the work itself.

YOUR OUTREACH ASSETS

Biblical Mandate

Shared, Explicit Faith

You Are a Community

People Resources

Fundraising Abilities

Understand Your Area

Contacts/Influence

Respect

Physical Facilities

Location/Visibility

Your Vision of Wholeness

Prayer circle at White Memorial Presbyterian, in Raleigh, North Carolina, includes families from Step-Up, White Memorial's transitional housing program.

Doing Something Specific

This is a book about how your congregation can love its neighbors in very concrete ways. While the book is intended to inspire as much as to inform, to celebrate as much as to describe, it's really a book about action. Its ultimate goal is to enable you to fashion your own successful outreach efforts, and its five sections are designed to help you do just that.

Possibilities to Consider

Success stories from across the country

POSSIBILITIES TO CONSIDER includes ideas and success stories from churches and synagogues nationwide (p. 9).

Insights into Outreach

Practical perspectives on important issues

INSIGHTS INTO OUTREACH features observations about outreach, with quotes from people interviewed (p. 99).

Getting Things to Happen

Making outreach a reality in your congregation

GETTING THINGS TO HAPPEN explains how to select and launch an outreach project (p. 129).

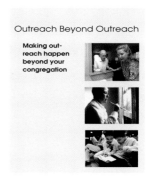

Outreach Beyond Outreach

Making outreach happen beyond your congregation

OUTREACH BEYOND OUTREACH explores making outreach extend even farther (p. 157).

Resources You Can Use

Where to find helpful people and information

RESOURCES includes contacts and references to help you get your efforts under way (p. 165).

Three Basic Questions

When you think about how you will make a difference, keep these three basic questions in mind:

Empowerment — or a band-aid?

As the proverb implies, teaching people to fish is generally preferable to giving them a fish. Empowerment is better than a band-aid. But it may not be an either-or choice; both may be needed in your community. Lets look at unemployment. Teaching job skills to unemployed people can make a lasting difference, but meals and shelter for the night can meet pressing needs of those who are out of work and unable to learn at the moment. If you do choose the band-aid approach, try to go beyond the day-to-day needs, for instance by referring people to job training or other sources of help in making fundamental changes in their lives.

Is there a "system" problem?

Some people may be out of work even though they have good work skills. One reason may be that there aren't enough jobs, and jobs may be scarce because there's no capital available for business start-ups. A scarcity of jobs is a "system" problem or "root cause" that needs fixing. It's like the bad curve in the road that causes accidents: the people who get injured need medical attention, but the curve needs to be removed so that no more people get hurt. Your congregation may want to focus on this kind of problem.

Service, community education, social action or advocacy?

Let's look at education this time. Your skills and resources may be well suited to direct service — an after-school program. But perhaps someone in your community should be doing other things — helping people understand the need for more or better schools; encouraging or organizing parents to take a public stand; and even advocating alongside them on behalf of the children. Perhaps, at some point, that "someone" will be your congregation.

"Give someone a fish and you feed them for a day, teach someone to fish and you feed them for a lifetime"

Chinese proverb

Soup kitchen or job training?

The Power of Numbers

Yours is one of a staggering number of churches and synagogues in this country — more than 330,000 — with a total membership of over 150 million people, more than all registered voters and equal to a good deal more than half our total population.

In fact, there are more churches and synagogues in America, by far, than any other kind of organization, and they have by far the largest combined membership.

Bound by a common purpose, your congregation and all the others have unprecedented potential as a force for good in our communities and beyond. If *every* congregation undertook *some* kind of outreach activity, we could make tremendous inroads on a great variety of problems. Here's just one example:

Building Habitat for Humanity Homes
Potential: 500,000 homes for low income people

Habitat for Humanity (see p. 65; also *Resources* section) is a program that pairs volunteers and financial contributions from congregations and others to build or refurbish homes side by side with low-income families both here and abroad; each family can own the home they helped build, at cost. Former President Jimmy Carter, so often pictured with a Habitat hammer in his hand, sees every congregation building one home, and larger congregations building several.

If just 50,000 congregations — one in six — did a Habitat project in a given year, over a period of 10 years a total of 500,000 homes would be built by churches and synagogues. And more than two million low-income people (equal to the combined populations of Boston and Philadelphia) would have wonderful, affordable homes.

Catching the Spirit of Outreach

People who have built a Habitat house, run a homeless shelter, started an after-school program, helped someone find a job — they all have a special something about them. You might call it the spirit of outreach.

Sometimes that spirit is obvious — in their enthusiastic telling of all the details about their program or project, the obstacles they've overcome, their hopes for the future. In other people there's a quieter, almost off-hand manner — they'll tell you they're not doing anything out of the ordinary, they're just doing what they know is right or merely acting out their faith.

If there's any doubt in your mind that your congregation should be doing some kind of outreach, or more of it, just visit with a few church or synagogue people who are doing it, and you will find the spirit of outreach strongly present — and very hard to resist!

High school students from a church in Saco, Maine, help out at a soup kitchen in Washington, D.C., as part of their "pilgrimage" program through Church of the Pilgrims in that city (see p. 88).

Possibilities to Consider

**Success Stories
from across the country**

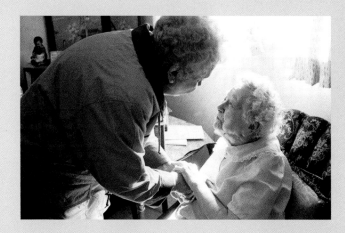

A vision without a task is a dream;
A task without a vision is drudgery;
A vision and a task is the hope of the world.

Anonymous

You're about to be introduced to a church that makes tractors to ship to farmers in Central America, a church that raises cattle as food for hungry people in the city, a synagogue and church that rehabilitated skid row hotels, a church that built housing units right in its own building, and another one that took to the streets to "finger" and shut down crack houses!

You may be thinking, "Way out!" But the fact is, they did these things, and they did them because they saw the needs, checked out the available resources, and found these to be appropriate responses.

These stories are included not because they would be appropriate for every church and synagogue but rather to show that there are many ways to do outreach, and some of them are unconventional. So be sure to remain open to any idea that may come into your mind!

Altogether, there are more than 100 outreach possibilities in the following pages. They will give you a smorgasbord of things to choose from — and also a kaleidoscope that, if you move it just a bit, may make you see a new possibility that's just right for the needs you see around you. In fact, in presenting these ideas, triggering your imagination to come up with yet another way, your way, is as important as providing you with models to use.

A Nationwide Search for Outreach Stories

There are literally thousands of wonderful stories out there. The research for this book spanned the country and turned up over 500 congregations involved in many kinds of outreach.

A Sampling of Possibilities for You

More than 70 stories were selected for presentation with photographs in this *Possibilities* section, under the eight headings shown on the next page. The central ideas of many other stories are included as "Other Possibilities" at the end of each group of feature stories.

Lay people and clergy were interviewed, and the great majority of the congregations featured were visited. Insights gained are presented later in the book.

The Congregations and the Projects

The stories come from Catholic, Protestant and Jewish congregations of all sizes, in urban, suburban and rural settings. The projects themselves are varied and include:

- Mostly neighborhood, community and metropolitan projects
- Primarily individual congregations, but also joint efforts
- Some interdenominational and interfaith examples
- Mostly "hands-on" projects
- A number of quite unusual undertakings

A Ninth Heading: Your Ideas

Remember that the possibilities in this section are only a sampling of the options your congregation will want to consider. As you read, if you think up new projects or recall others you've heard of, jot them down on p. 97.

INDEX OF POSSIBILITIES

Things to think about as you read

- What are the needs in our community or beyond?
- Is there a need for the project I'm reading about?
- Is it appealing to me as something to do?
- Does it look possible for our congregation to do alone?
- If not, might we do it with another congregation or organization?
- Is there a special twist I can think of to make it a better fit for us?
- Is there something else we might do that's not included here? If so include it in your ideas list on p. 97.

Care and Access

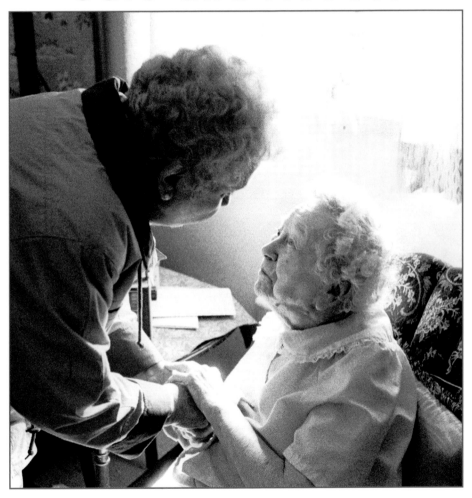

Warm, interested and capable — your congregation has lots of people like that. There's lots for them to do, since your community, and probably your own congregation, has people who are lonely or sick or homebound; people who have immediate needs for money or other help; people who face barriers they're unable to overcome.

Providing companionship and lending a hand in times of need can be hugely important forms of service. They offer wonderful opportunities both for people who want the deep rewards of working one-on-one and for those with a talent for organizing.

Then there's access. Barriers in our society exist for many — for example, people who have physical limitations, speak only a language other than English, come from a different culture, or have a prison record. Even the entrance stairs to your congregation's own building may be barriers to some people. Eliminating barriers is an excellent inreach/outreach project. It can include a larger community in the active worship, life and work of your congregation, while meeting very real needs in your community.

Since so much of this type of outreach can be done solely by volunteers, many projects will cost your congregation very little. So, if you have a terrific idea, it's likely the resources can be found. However you design your approach, it starts and grows with your greatest resource of all: the warm, interested and capable people in your congregation.

Helping the Homebound Helps a Church Merger and Yields Job Skills as Well
Church of the Resurrection, Omaha, Nebraska

This church is the result of a merger of two declining congregations, one African-American, one white. To stay focused on being one congregation, the church decided to work on the needs of the frail elderly in Omaha. Many were at risk of having to enter nursing homes prematurely because there was much they could no longer do on their own at home. Many services were available for this population, but few knew how to obtain them.

Church member Nona Taylor, a professional social worker, helped the church ask the University of Nebraska's Department of Gerontology to design and provide a 12-week training program. Nine dedicated volunteers from the church learned how to assess needs, be advocates and coordinate services. In the first five years, over 1,000 homebound elderly people were served! Thirty-two volunteers now work in the program, including volunteers from outside the church.

There was also a great need for homemaker services. Many clients couldn't afford the high private rates charged by homecare companies, but they had too much income to qualify for public homecare. In a stroke of genius, Ms. Taylor hit upon the idea of training welfare mothers to provide homemaker services for the elderly as private contractors. The homemakers charge less than companies, and they enjoy the advantage of being able to set their own hours. The church simply provides the training and referrals, and makes the connections. Recently, 42 new homemakers entered the program in a single year.

"We didn't want to turn inward, end up arguing about how the two groups served communion or what songs we sang. So we tried to find ways to keep our energy flowing outward on a single mission."

Church member Nona Taylor

Training Volunteer Social Workers to Meet Emergency and Other Needs
First United Methodist Church, Huntsville, Alabama

It looks like an expensive operation. In fact, the whole undertaking costs the church very little because it's run by volunteers. By training church members to be social workers, First United Methodist Church stretches the very limited power of its small welfare fund to meet the needs "that just come in off the street".

First they recruited a dozen volunteers willing to make a substantial time commitment. Then they established a 3-month training program in basic social work using professional social workers and a clinical psychologist.

Other church members identified every possible source of help and compiled them into an exhaustive list of color-coded resource files. Then they taught the volunteers how to use the files to make referrals.

Two Decades of Elder Care in the Church's House
Christ Lutheran Church, Bethesda, Maryland

It's quiet and clean and peaceful when you walk into Bethesda Fellowship House, Christ Lutheran's adult day care center. Elders come on the van or are brought by family. One of the staff usually greets the elders, hangs up their coats, helps them to seats in the bright, comfortable living room.

Some people talk with each other, some people pace (a symptom of Alzheimer's) if they need to. There are good smells and comforting clinking noises coming from the kitchen as the staff dietician makes them coffee and muffins. In a little while it's time for current events, where a staff person reads the newspaper headlines to the group in the sun room.

"Twenty years ago hardly anybody had heard of adult day care," says program Sarah Nichols. But in 1972, while looking for a way to use a house on their property, members of the church saw a clear need for that type of care in the community.

At 10 a.m. it's time for coffee hour. A staffer points to a free seat in the dining room at Bethesda House

Today about 35 adults use the 23-person licensed facility (not all come every day). There's a two-month waiting list. About 60% have Alzheimer's or a similar disease.

The doors are open weekdays from 7:30 a.m. to 5:30 p.m. This means the care-giver in the family can have a full-time job, and 40% do. Most of the other caregivers are the retired spouses.

There's a professional staff, one person for each four adults, and a sliding scale of fees. The church provides the house rent-free and, at the moment, the liability insurance as well. Some church members volunteer to assist the staff. All this enables the cost to participants to be kept between $30 to $40 a day.

The state provides a grant for low income people for a total of about 1,000 days of care each year, which allows four to five people to be accommodated. Depending on one's income, the daily cost can be as low as $3. Fees are also kept down by the federally funded county nutrition program, which brings in a warm lunch daily.

In another house on its property, Christ Lutheran provides infant day care. State and county assistance and some scholarships from the congregation keep costs as low as six dollars a day for about eight of the 62 children.

Church financial support for both day care programs comes from a bazaar held each year.

SHARE Encourages Caring by Exchanging Community Service for a Bargain in Food

St. Gerard Majella Church, Canton, Massachusetts

SHARE is a way to expand community service far beyond your congregation's volunteer resources. Inspired by Mother Teresa, SHARE (Self Help and Resource Exchange) is a way for communities to promote volunteer work by stretching food dollars. The idea is catching on nationwide.

For just two volunteer hours a month, plus about $13 in cash or food stamps, volunteers receive meat, produce and staples worth $30-$35. The food is high quality, not surplus, but is bargain priced because SHARE buys in quantity at a deep discount. Everybody qualifies — there are no age or income requirements.

Volunteers come from your own congregation and the community. They serve the community through their church or synagogue or a school or social service program, by helping a neighbor, or by doing SHARE program work.

Your congregation coordinates the program and makes service opportunities known. With other volunteers, your members bag the food and bring it from the warehouse. Your church or synagogue is the "host site" where all volunteers come to pick up their food and offer proof of their community service.

SHARE is rapidly expanding. St. Gerard's is but one of many congregations all over the country with SHARE programs. See the *Resources* section for the SHARE office near you; staff will be glad to tell you how to start a program.

Community service voucher from another area church.

St. Gerard's volunteers check the list of SHARE participants to make sure that everyone has come to pick up their food.

Young people at St. Gerard's get involved helping people load the monthly food package in their cars.

Making their Church "User Friendly" for People with Disabilities

Newman Congregational Church, United Church of Christ, of Seakonk and East Providence, Rhode Island

What started as a study of the feasibility of a wheelchair ramp eventually turned into a major focus of the congregation's life at the Newman Congregational Church, UCC. "We wanted to remove one of the barriers that we erect that exclude people with disabilities." says Pastor David F. Shire, "We found out how many barriers we had."

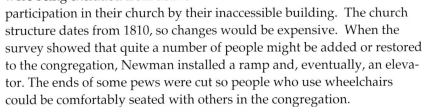

"We have simply tried to make the church a user friendly place. We have a far more diverse congregation. That is a real gift to all of us."

Reverend David Shire

The congregation did a survey in 1982 to see how many people were being excluded from active participation in their church by their inaccessible building. The church structure dates from 1810, so changes would be expensive. When the survey showed that quite a number of people might be added or restored to the congregation, Newman installed a ramp and, eventually, an elevator. The ends of some pews were cut so people who use wheelchairs could be comfortably seated with others in the congregation.

Newman's cut away pews allow people in wheelchairs to sit with the rest of the congregation.

The church also began to consider who else might be shut out by other kinds of barriers. The pastor discovered that there was one married couple who regularly attended the church, leaving their severely disabled child at home because she couldn't be accommodated by the church school program. A multi-disciplinary team, put together with help from a nearby Easter Seal school, spent a full year designing a program accessible to kids with mental, emotional and physical disabilities.

In time, this concern for access led the church to have someone "sign" for the deaf at worship services. The signer worked one Sunday each month for a year and a half and not a single deaf person attended. The church decided to continue the effort because they felt they should and because they had grown to appreciate the beauty of communicating by signing. Two weeks later, four deaf people came. Now every other Sunday includes signing.

The signer, Christine Dunleavy, teaches Reverend Shire (right) and congregation members to sign.

Taking Children to See Their Mothers in Prison

St. Anne's Parish, Barrington, Illinois

It doesn't take lots of energy from the church or a lot of money, but the caring volunteers from St. Anne's Parish make an enormous difference in the lives of some mothers and their children separated from each other by prison walls.

The visits are often the only opportunities that mothers in the prison get to see their children. One of the visits in the summer lasts for an entire weekend. The children also become a link between their mothers and their family and neighborhood.

The program was organized by Lutheran Family Advocacy, a social service agency in Chicago, working with Sister Lorraine Menheer, who coordinates the church's many outreach efforts.

Because of all the driving (three hours round-trip from Barrington to Chicago and five hours round-trip to and from the prison), and then the time needed for the visit, it is an immense 11 to 12 hour day for the volunteers. Most of them find it worth every bit of the effort.

Catholic Church of St. Anne's volunteers arrive after one and a half hours on the road to load up the van with children going to see their mothers in prison, another two and a half hours away. The children live in the buildings in the background.

Sponsoring Nearly Two Hundred Refugees in Eighteen Years

Zion Evangelical Lutheran Church, Bristol, Connecticut

top: the three-family house bought by members of the congregation to house refugees until they find their own place. above: members of the congregation and of two of the families they have sponsored.

Their work started in 1975 when a small group of volunteers at Zion Lutheran started putting aside $10-$15 each a week to help refugees from Vietnam. That year, the volunteers urged the church to sponsor two refugee brothers to come to this country. That small beginning has led to the church's sponsorship of nearly 200 refugees from seven different countries.

The former parsonage is used as housing for some of the refugees until they can get their own place. Others live in a three-family house next door, bought by members of the congregation.

All of the refugees, in time, have found jobs, homes, and a place in American life. Some have joined the church. Most continue to have regular ties to the church community.

> *"...it is healthy to share life with people of a different color. It has broken down the distinction between 'us' and 'them.'"*
>
> **Associate in Ministry**
>
> **Shirley Dickau**

Other Possibilities:

Our Lady of the Woods, Woodland Park, Colorado, a church in a small town at the foot of Pike's Peak, has a **network of volunteers** on call to help out in times of need.

St. Mark's Catholic Church, Boise, Idaho, has a **crisis action center** in a separate building that grew out of its St. Jude's Fund. People can come to the center for help with food, rent, utilities and transportation, and for referrals. A unique feature is the "Night Riders," a group of parishioners on call who offer help anonymously as much as possible.

Community Baptist Church, Milwaukee, Wisconsin, helps families by offering **affordable day care and pre-school programs** that accept non-financial contributions. Parents may volunteer to help out, assist in fundraising, even provide peanut butter cookies they have made.

Ridge Evangelical Lutheran Church, Chicago, Illinois, is another church that hired a signer for the hearing impaired at their worship services. Having gone through a discernment process to focus its community ministries (as part of the Church and Community Project at McCormick Theological Seminary) concern and understanding of the congregation blossomed into a city-wide **advocacy effort for the deaf and hearing impaired**. Supported by a Lilly Foundation grant, the advocacy succeeded in getting hospitals, police and fire departments to be responsive to the needs and rights of people with hearing impairments.

First Baptist Church, Fresno, California, **helped Asian immigrants start their own congregation** as part of their extensive assistance efforts for newcomers.

St. Luke Presbyterian Church in Wayzata, Minnesota, provided space on its property for a "sweat lodge" for worship as part of its **hospitality to Native Americans**.

St. Jules Catholic Church, Lafayette, Louisiana, a predominantly white parish, has formed a relationship with another Catholic church that is almost totally African-American. Members of both congregations have shared a **retreat to discuss racial justice** issues. Great communication has happened and wonderful friendships have been formed.

New ideas of your own?
Projects you like?
Jot them down on p. 97.

Food and Shelters

GARDENING
FOR
GOD

A meal and a bed can make all the difference to someone who has neither. Offering a warm, welcoming setting in which to eat or sleep is a real gift to a hungry or homeless person.

Congregations have traditionally fed the hungry and sheltered the homeless. Unfortunately there is greater need than ever for shelter for the homeless and food for the hungry, and congregations have an important role to play in filling these needs.

Volunteers at Community Baptist Church in Milwaukee, Wisconsin, welcome hungry people for breakfast.

Often, however, a person who is hungry or homeless has needs that go beyond food and shelter. Providing assistance in finding work, medical care, legal aid and housing along with a meal or a bed can make a more lasting difference.

If your church or synagogue isn't where the needs are, you may want to connect with one that is, so your members can volunteer their time to serve in the soup kitchen or shelter, provide professional services, or help in other ways.

If you want to have a shelter in your own building, it might be a rotating one with other congregations also taking turns hosting people one night a week or, preferably, one week at a time. Another option is a season-long shelter. Local agencies can provide screened candidates for you. Still other ways to help include: operating a food pantry, distributing clothing, and preparing food or growing it on land your congregation or its members own. You might even raise beef cattle to ship to the city, as St. Joseph's does!

Starting a Bakery
Seventh Day Adventist Church, Barberton, Ohio

Sharing the storefront space of this church's community center is a bakery. Church member Kathy Swanson spends three days a week baking the organic bread and other wares of the New Start Bakery. Some of the bread is sold with profits going toward the budget of the center, some is used for school lunches, and the rest is simply given away, along with other food, to those who need it.

Provisions come from an area-wide food bank, with the center paying only 10 cents per pound for whatever it needs. All of the other items are donated with regularity by members of the church and other people in the community.

As volunteer assistant director Helen Burza says: "We keep giving food away and worrying where more will come from, but more just keeps coming in. You just can't outgive the Lord." Emergency financial resources come out of the church's outreach budget.

Raising Chickens and Black Angus
St. Joseph's Parish, Apple Creek, Missouri

St. Joseph's Parish is in the midst of prosperous farm country, in a small town about 85 miles south of St. Louis. "We really don't have many needy people in the area of our parish," says Father Joseph Bolderson, "but people here have been very moved by what they've heard of needy people in the city."

In a parish full of farmers and gardeners, that concern turned into an effort by "virtually everyone in the parish" to grow a few extra rows of vegetables in their gardens for people in nearby urban areas.

The young people of the church are raising 50 chickens on church property (the process serves as a science project as well).

The parish also fenced off a four-acre parcel of its beautiful 40 acre site to raise cattle—two Black Angus steers named Origen and Abelard, which were eventually slaughtered and their meat sent to people in need in St. Charles and St. Louis.

"We feel like it's a way to say thank you for all of the blessings of our lives here in this beautiful place," says Father Bolderson.

Mounting a Massive Program to Help a Multitude
Church of the Holy Apostles, New York, New York

"Our mission endures, as challenging as it is compelling . . . to keep open the doors of hope for all who are in need." This is the way Rector William A. Greenlaw speaks about the efforts of his church to care for the hungry and homeless in what is now the second largest soup kitchen in the country.

In 1982, Holy Apostles opened its doors to provide meals for a few homeless men whom parishioners saw across the street. The church served about 35 meals. To date, they have served two million.

The line for the Holy Apostles soup kitchen in Manhattan, New York, wraps around the block.

The line begins to form in front of the church before 8:00 a.m. It is a line of people who are sick, disabled, homeless, or elderly. By the time the doors open at 10:30 a.m., the line stretches for almost three blocks. Things move quickly, for in three hours the church will feed over 1,000 people a hot, nutritious meal in a space that seats only 70 at a time. A small army of volunteers from all over the city and suburbs, along with 21 full and part-time staff members—some of them formerly homeless people themselves—work with impressive efficiency to serve six people per minute. No questions are asked. Anyone is welcome to come and receive a meal. No one is ever turned away, no matter how many arrive.

Soon it will be possible to serve larger numbers at a more leisurely pace because the church decided to host the diners right in the sanctuary which has been outfitted with movable "cathedral" seats in a restoration project.

While the sheer numbers and overwhelming need are daunting, Holy Apostles does not stop at "just" a soup kitchen. There is an extensive counseling and referral service that assists 75 people each week with obtaining job training, drug and alcohol rehabilitation, permanent housing, clothing, and social security. There is an on-site legal clinic provided each week by the Legal Action Center for the Homeless. Three times a week, there is an on-site health clinic operated by the Manhattan Bowery Project. There are also support groups for guests seeking solutions to a wide range of problems.

"We are in a daily battle for people's lives here," said a counselor in the program. In the midst of a homeless population estimated at 100,000 in the city of New York alone, Holy Apostles—despite the huge numbers it serves—is just one church desperately trying to be faithful to the call to love its neighbors. The result is inspiring. Hundreds of people from the metropolitan area now come to volunteer as part of this one small church's effort to live out its faith. As Development Director Kami O'Keeffe put it, "If poverty is a battlefield...this has quickly become the front lines."

A Church with a Mission that Includes Haircuts, Showers, Even Greeting Cards
Fort Street Presbyterian Church, Detroit, Michigan

"Come here on Thursday morning and you'll not only get an eyeful, you'll get a heart full," says Reverend Robert Crilley. For 26 years, Fort Street has been a place of hope and care for the down-and-out.

The Open Door program was conceived as a service to senior citizens, but very quickly those who needed it most—what Reverend Crilley calls the "flotsam and jetsam of Detroit's streets"—became the main focus of its work. The program is simple. "In one place, at one time, we offer a complete cafeteria of services for people who live on the streets," says the pastor. Every Thursday, over 800 people come to find a variety of help.

On hand each week are doctors and nurses for health screening and treatment, funded by the Robert Wood Johnson Foundation. There are also dentists, three barbers, and an optometrist. There are showers, used clothing, a full meal, and food to go. A veterans' affairs official is also on hand. There is even a greeting card table and someone to help people write cards and letters.

Volunteer Paul Van Ermen signs someone up for clothing.

Reverend Crilley and others keep all of this going by visiting Presbyterian churches in the Detroit area and asking for money. Over 60 urban and suburban churches lend financial and other support. As he says, "If churches don't start doing more of this work, it won't be done by anybody. We have to pick up the burden that no one else wants, because that's what the church is here for."

The Fort Street congregation has been enhanced by all of this. The church has become a "metropolitan" congregation. As Reverend Crilley puts it, "People will go past a dozen other churches to get to us because they know that this is a church with a mission."

A Legal Residence
St. Luke's Episcopal Church, Atlanta, Georgia

Cluade Carlton (left) and Bill Jones enjoy a meal at St. Luke's.

Like Holy Apostles and Fort Street, St. Luke's too has a soup kitchen, which serves 600 homeless people each day. People also get counseling and referrals, and through the Atlanta Enterprise Center, they get job readiness training, housing and other assistance, all geared to make them self-sufficient.

But St. Luke's also tackles one of homeless people's biggest problems: not having an address. If you are not a "resident" with an address, you can't register to vote and may not be able to get benefits you are otherwise entitled to. Over 3,000 people living on Atlanta's streets use St. Luke's as their legal residence. A full-time staff person and several volunteers run a computerized mail room where people can receive their mail. Help with voter registration is provided periodically.

A Daytime Shelter and Daytime and Evening Drop-In Centers
Cass Community United Methodist Church, Detroit, Michigan

Reverend Edwin A. Rowe, the effective, self-described "ordained beggar"

When Pastor Ed Rowe was asked how his 140 member urban church is able to do all that it does, his answer was simple: "Everybody here has a sense of mission. We know that we are called to be faithful."

That sense of mission sustains an amazing amount of work on behalf of a vast poor and homeless population in the "Cass Corridor" neighborhood of Detroit. The Cass Community Church serves over three thousand meals a week; the Saturday lunches are provided by suburban churches. Every Saturday the church also provides a free medical clinic.

While homeless people from the area are transported many nights to other churches which rotate sheltering responsibilities during the week, it is to Cass's drop-in center that they come each day to do laundry, take showers, find clothing, and keep their belongings. They also come for referrals and for the opportunity for literacy training and basic English and math education through volunteer teachers.

Cass not only tries to care for the homeless, but has also raised both block grant funds and private resources to rehabilitate two area apartment buildings into housing for low-income people. After a number of years, a third project is still struggling for lack of public funds.

Cass also provides recreation, education and entertainment in a daytime and evening drop-in center for 130 developmentally disabled adults. Frail elderly persons also receive services in their homes from Cass outreach workers, and another group of elderly come to the church each day for a traditional senior activity center. The church also has a clothing closet to provide clothing to low income people and those with emergency needs.

Cass's various projects involve many volunteers and community service workers including people from the Urban League, senior citizens and Peter Claver Center workers. But the church also employs 50 paid staff people, partly supported by the county mental health board and organizations for the homeless. 'How do you get the rest of the money for all of this?' the pastor was asked. "I beg. I'm an ordained beggar. And there's not a church east or west that doesn't give or participate here in some way." It was hard to get in touch with Reverend Rowe because he spends much of his time at Michigan's State House also begging, that something be done for the people at the center of his church's ministry.

The bus used to transport the homeless to night shelter at other churches, with Cass Church in the background.

Christians, Jews Create Community-Wide Shelter

First Church Congregational, Fairfield, Connecticut

These days, even in affluent communities like Fairfield, Connecticut, homelessness has become a challenge for caring churches and synagogues. By coming together cooperatively, as First Church co-pastor David Spollett says, "we could mount an effort beyond anything we could have accomplished singly."

Back in 1985 at a local clergy association meeting, several Jewish and Christian clergy reported receiving sharply increasing numbers of appeals for food, shelter, and money. Clergy members went on to discuss their perceptions with their congregations, and everyone seemed to agree that an organized response was needed.

In the meantime, First Church Congregational decided simply to open its doors when someone came seeking shelter. The first night, the church sheltered just one man. Within weeks, up to 15 men were sleeping in a church corridor where there was a restroom, using cushions and bed rolls that church members had scraped together. As church people got more involved with these homeless people, they realized that many additional services and resources were needed.

Members of the clergy started to meet with the town's selectmen, who were anxious to develop a creative response, and after some time Operation Hope was born. The town provided, for one dollar a year, its old police station building, with heat and utilities. The churches and synagogues set out to raise the money for extensive

renovation and the hiring of staff. It took a full year to accomplish the renovation, but that year was well used in public hearings and helping the neighborhood to accept the project. "Not in my backyard" opposition was kept to a minimum.

Currently, Operation Hope includes a shelter for men, a shelter for women, a daytime drop-in program for the homeless, a food pantry, and a community kitchen that serves hot meals to all comers every night. The program also spends much effort on rehabilitative services, including health care, job-seeking assistance, emotional and substance abuse counseling, transportation help, and referrals.

Most of the financial support, and the hundreds of volunteers that make the program work, still

Where it all started: Co-Pastor David Spollett with former Social Action chair Jeanne Lee in the church hallway.

Fairfield's former police station has been converted into Operation Hope, a shelter for people who are homeless.

come from those 15 churches and synagogues whose compassion got things started, but now the whole community is involved. A well attended joint choir concert every year raises over $20,000 for Operation Hope.

A Week-At-A-Time Shelter

Kitchell Memorial Presbyterian Church, East Hanover, New Jersey

Kitchell is one of 12 churches in Morris County that, in rotation, take in up to 20 homeless people for a week, four times a year. Screened by the county's Interfaith Council for Homeless Families, the guests arrive by van from the previous host church on a Sunday afternoon. The church will already have set up partitions so that each family has a private space. Partitions have "welcome" signs on them, and the partitioned spaces give a real feeling of privacy, of "turf."

Guests eat in the parish hall. For showers, they go to a home-type bathroom in the church offices

left: a welcome sign for the night's guests. above: coordinator Peg Gruenz.

in a small house next door. The whole feeling of the place and the operation is intimate and inviting. In large measure, this is due not just to the physical set-up but to the many warm volunteers: more than half the

congregation's members have been involved in some way! But its success is also because it's extremely well coordinated by Peg Gruenz, an empathetic volunteer: "These are mostly very proud people that come to us for shelter. They just want to be considered as human beings and treated that way. I've been brought down to earth by these people; my problems seem small compared to what they are handling."

One of the advantages of the program is that it exposes a great many volunteers to the problem of homelessness, and they often become strong advocates for change. Dozens of people at Kitchell are now part of a phone chain that responds with calls and letters when any housing related issue is being considered by a government body. As Peg says, "This is just a temporary stop-gap, the best we can do right now. It is not a solution; we have to find a solution."

A Season-Long Night Shelter, Pressure for Housing, and "Moving On"

Congregation Rodeph Sholom, New York, New York

Like many large urban congregations, Rodeph Sholom reaches out in a variety of ways to care for the needy in the city. For homeless men they have a rather unusual program: a season-long shelter right in the main building. In the early evening, five nights a week from October to May, homeless men enter the main doors of the synagogue and mount the marble stairs to a spacious, eight-bed room with its own small kitchen. The guests have been screened by an agency whose day shelter they attend. Some come every night, for the whole season.

The congregation provides clean beds, stocks a refrigerator with food for evening snacks and breakfast, and, as lawyer and volunteer shelter coordinator Jay Kranis says, "most important, a warm and welcoming atmosphere." There's a TV set available just outside the door. Sometimes the men want to talk with the volunteers, sometimes not; the volunteers respect the men's wishes. It's Jay's key job to assure that each night there's a two-person team of volunteers who take turns sleeping in a chapel just down the hall from the men. A number of families have served, often bringing their young children to help out and stay the night.

The experience of working directly with the homeless men has motivated the temple to form a coalition of West Side synagogues — Reform, Conservative, Orthodox, and Reconstructionist — to apply political pressure on the city to increase its efforts to find permanent housing solutions for the homeless.

Another, more modest program, but a very caring one, is called "Moving On." Packages of basic necessities are assembled and distributed to homeless families who are finally able to move into apartments. The packages include a large amount of basic foodstuffs, a set of dishes, flatware, an assortment of pots and pans, some toys for the kids, and even plants to brighten up the new space. "There is a lot of attention directed to the needs of the homeless," says Rabbi Robert Levine, "but often, once a family finds a place to live, people assume that the problem is solved. But there are many needs for people moving into a new home. We try to fill them."

The shelter stays well stocked for snacks and breakfast.

Volunteer Dan Nichols makes his bed in the chapel.

Other Possibilities:

Food pantries, clothing closets, and basic soup kitchens are so common that they're not featured here with individual stories. Yet they are very important services for you to consider. Check with another congregation in your area to find out how they have set up theirs.

Like St. Joseph's your congregation may be lucky enough to have enough land to farm for food to give away, sell for the benefit of the needy, or serve in your soup kitchen. But even the yard of your church or synagogue can be used to grow food: indeed, in Cleveland **a church grows food on its front lawn** in a vegetable garden yielding 2,400 pounds a season! Or **your congregants may have land to "garden for God,"** donating produce to area soup kitchens.

Finally, your members may have **crop land which people can "glean"** for what is left after the harvest. All that's necessary is to let local soup kitchens, shelters, or social service agencies know about available land.

University Baptist Church, Seattle, Washington, has worked with six other churches to organize a **rotating shelter for teenagers** who live on the streets.

Church of the Pilgrims, Washington, D.C., established "Elizabeth House" at an undisclosed location as a **home for five pregnant homeless women**. The church provides a live-in volunteer house manager.

Calvary by the Sea Lutheran Church, Honolulu, Hawaii, has an **"angel" network of volunteers who support homeless people** living in five "Ohana" houses the church leases. "Ohana" is Hawaiian for extended family, and that's how the church thinks of the homeless. This church "by the sea" has a unique way of supporting the network. A large, hollow whale sculpture graces the inside of the church. In special services, members who "have experienced great blessings" come forward, share their stories, and place a thank offering in the whale. In one year the whale raised $122,000 for the program; a single community auction raised $50,000 more!

New ideas of your own?
Projects you like?
Jot them down on p. 97.

Health and Well-Being

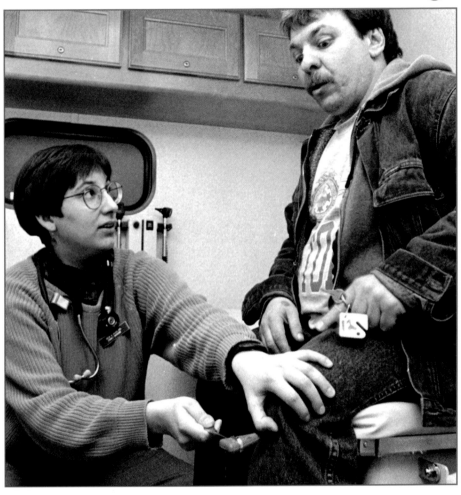

If you don't feel well, it's hard to build a home, go to an after-school program, hold a job or look for one, or do just about anything else. Creating a healthy spirit is a congregation's forte; helping people stay healthy in body and mind can also fill real needs in your community.

Your church or synagogue might be an excellent setting for a medical clinic for people who need care but are uninsured or too poor to pay. Doctors and other professionals may be available from your own congregation or recruited from your community.

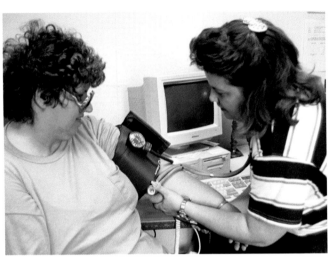

A volunteer nurse takes blood pressure at a free clinic run on Wednesday nights by St. Andrew's Episcopal Church in Barboursville, West Virginia.

People may need to see a specialist in order to get the right treatment but can't afford to do it. One church created a community-wide network of specialists who offer free office visits.

Mental illness and AIDS are also important areas that need the involvement of caring people. Mental illness is still afforded an uneasy status in much of our society, with people often receiving less sympathy, understanding or help than those with a physical illness. AIDS patients are feared and shunned by many, instead of being loved and cared for.

There are myriad ways your congregation can get involved with the physical and mental health of your community. With uneven access to care and health costs still on the rise, outreach in this area can have a real and lasting impact.

A Health Clinic, a "Remarkable and Moving Scene" and Much, Much More

Central Presbyterian Church, Atlanta, Georgia

"When so many of the other churches were leaving the inner city, way back in the 1920s, this church decided to stay and minister with the people right here. Even then, that meant the poor." Reverend Agnes Norfleet is talking about the beginnings of a commitment on the part of Central Presbyterian, the oldest piece of which is still going on.

In 1922, the church founded a well baby clinic to provide basic medical care for children living in poverty in the city. Today that clinic has grown into the Central Health Center. Still housed in the church building, the Center serves over 6,000 patients a year. It provides basic treatment, physical exams, family planning, immunizations, dental care, a pharmacy, and individual and family counseling. The Center is directed by a doctor with a staff of a nurse practitioner, two other nurses, a part-time dentist, and a lab technician. Patients are charged on a sliding scale. For those in serious need, services are free.

Once a week, a remarkable and moving scene takes place at the shelter that Central Presbyterian has run for homeless people since 1981. Every Wednesday night there is a "foot clinic." The most pressing medical need of the homeless population is care for feet that get no rest and little protection. During the foot clinic, a large crew of volunteers comes in to wash and soak the residents' feet and treat cuts and callouses. On the same night, the Health Center, staffed with volunteer doctors and nurses, offers services to the shelter population.

When asked how the church supports all of these efforts, Reverend Norfleet says, "When we have the greatest needs, donations of money and time have simply come, like manna from heaven." The church remains strong, and one of the reasons is their "pride in our long tradition of serving this community in a way that speaks our faith."

Central Presbyterian's weekly foot clinic treats cuts and callouses on the feet of homeless people.

Opening the Doors to the Doctor's Office
All Saints Episcopal Church, Pasadena, California

All Saints' 1983 centennial was really the beginning. The church had commissioned Denise Wood, a parishioner, writer and sociologist, to study the community, its strengths and problems.

Out of that study came the idea for OCC, an "Office for Creative Connections" that would identify urban needs and bring together coalitions of concerned individuals, organizations, and agencies to work on collaborative solutions.

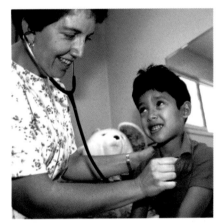

Getting a check-up through the Young and Healthy program.

Two further studies, and many meetings with the community, clarified a major need: providing access to expert health care for the one-third of all Pasadena young people who can't afford it. In 1988 the OCC convened the Health Coalition for Children and Youth, bringing together a wide cross section of the community that could help: the local

"If we could widen the doorway of each doctor's office, every needy child could get through."

Dr. J. Donald Thomas,

Coalition Chair

hospital, public health department, school district, a city commission on children and youth, physicians, mental health professionals, nurses, educators, community leaders and volunteers.

By 1990 the Coalition had developed the Young and Healthy program. The basic idea is that if many health professionals in the community would each volunteer free services in their offices for just a few children, then a significant amount of free care could be provided without burdening individual practitioners. Many health professionals have volunteered and are among the program's most enthusiastic supporters. As OCC's current director, Lorna Miller, says, "Our providers do more for these children than we have asked of them."

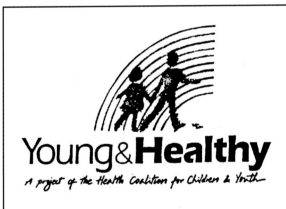

Through OCC, Young and Healthy receives grants from many sources. Mary Donnelly-Crocker, program director of Young and Healthy operates almost entirely with the aid of volunteers, and the school district donates office space. All Saints continues to provide substantial in-kind contributions as well. Young and Healthy in mid-1993 had over 200 participating professionals and 26 participating schools. In the 1992-93 academic year it provided 1,205 free office visits and numerous hours of volunteer time. These figures continue to rise.

Besides the needed care, tangible benefits include: improved school attendance, increased parent participation in school activities, and reduced need for acute care because preventive treatment is offered early. Harvard's Healthy Children program has enthusiastically endorsed the program as a model for communities to follow.

Meeting Mental Illness Needs in the Congregation and the Community
Church of the Risen Savior, Albuquerque, New Mexico

In this large suburban parish, people with mental illnesses and their families are the focus of a unique ministry. Originating in one woman's need for support in coping with a son's mental illness, the ministry has grown to include a full-time coordinator who helps the one in four families struggling with such illnesses. The program features two regularly scheduled interfaith programs, drawing volunteers and participants from several city congregations for faith sharing, support and friendship.

One is a two-hour program called "Afternoon Reflections," every other month, for parents and friends of people with mental illness. "It's very traumatic to live with and deal with — the families need a lot of support, " says Marge Cooney, parishioner and full time staff member who coordinates the program.

Anywhere from 40 to 90 people come from as far away as 60 miles to hear presentations on topics such as: Relating to Someone with Schizophrenia, The Good News about Depression, Coping with Holiday Blues. There is also a lot of time for group dynamics at small tables where people, maybe for the first time, have spoken to someone else about the mental illness they're dealing with in the family.

"Many who attend have had a problem in their family, maybe for years and years, but never sought help or are even aware there is any," says Ms. Cooney. While there's a local Alliance for the Mentally Ill support group, many family members prefer the church: "They feel on more friendly ground, when it's in a church. All kinds of things come out; there's never silence."

At the Faith & Friendship support group for people with mental illness, Marge Cooney (left) shares a moment with an attendee.

The other program, "Faith and Friendship", is a monthly one for people who have the illnesses. Many have no other social interaction that isn't therapy-based or mental health center-based; Risen Savior's program draws them into a faith community where they "have the opportunity to share faith with others." Half of the 37 who come have chronic mental illness and are drawn from the Alliance group in town; the other half are volunteers from churches.

The first of their two Sunday afternoon hours is devoted to a speaker or video on a topic such as self-esteem or life's limitations. There is also clarification of the true causes of mental illness: says Ms. Cooney, "Some people in some churches still preach today that demons cause schizophrenia!"

There's always a lot of discussion. "The really moving thing is that these people who have suffered so much also have so much to offer because of it. It's amazing the depths of feeling and insight they have!" At the end of the afternoon there's a sit-down dinner with candles, flowers and grace before and after. Everybody usually contributes something to it.

Many people usually show up for Afternoon Reflections, a gathering time for people who know or are related to people with mental illness.

Restoring Their Church, and the Health of the Homeless
Central Congregational Church, Providence, Rhode Island

"We couldn't just do bricks and mortar for ourselves with all that need out there." This is how church pastor Rebecca Spencer expresses her congregation's feelings about a 1990 capital fund drive to raise over a million dollars to restore their beautiful 19th century basilica in celebration of the building's centennial. Some of the money went into a traveling health ministry for the homeless.

Bob, the van's driver and a retired police officer, signs a man in to see the doctor for a back problem.

Central Church was the initial contributor, of $30,000, toward the purchase of a large new van to provide primary health care, mental health services, and substance abuse services to the homeless. Each weekday evening, from 6:00 to 10:00 p.m., the fully equipped, sleek mobile care unit is driven to all of the places where homeless people congregate in Providence. Sometimes it's outside a soup kitchen, and sometimes it's on a street corner.

On a cold winter's night, the van pulls up outside the Salvation Army, a welcome sight ready to take care of people there. Inside the van are professionals ready to talk with people, help heal their ailments, and make referrals. Many of those served stop in to pick up vitamin packs and aspirin provided, along with other medicines, by a local pharmacy.

The medical van spends one night a week outside the Salvation Army shelter for homeless men.

The driver, Bob, a retired policeman, tells waiting patients about the old van: "Boy, that thing was a dinosaur! It had a propane heater that kept going out; when it did work it was smelly and LOUD! And the van was about half this size."

The new van was equipped by the Travelers Aid Society of Providence, which operates and garages it. Federal funds cover costs of supplies and operation. The medical staff are volunteers. The van, with Travelers Aid and the name of the church and other contributors painted on the side, has now become a familiar sight around the city.

With its consciousness raised by this and a number of other projects for the homeless, Central Congregational is now building a Habitat for Humanity house, a real hands-on mission project, and sees more possibilities for the future. As Reverend Spencer describes people's reactions, "We are proud of what our church is becoming."

AIDS: Educating the Community
Unitarian Church of All Souls, New York, New York

AIDS is in many ways the modern equivalent of leprosy — a disease which can make its victims into untouchables because it is so feared and misunderstood. Reaching out to touch people regarded as untouchables has always been a special province of religious leaders and faith commu-

nities. But many congregations still fear involvement with people with AIDS. To counter this, All Souls' AIDS Task Force mounted a public education program that funds an AIDS newsletter and has placed 10,000 posters in city buses and subways with messages such as: "AIDS is a human disease and deserves a humane response," "AIDS: the more you understand, the more understanding you'll be," and the one shown at left.

A Residence for People with AIDS
Christ Episcopal Church, Raleigh, North Carolina

Having recently supported his own daughter through a close friend's struggle with AIDS, former rector Daniel Sapp decided to use sabbatical time to explore how other churches were ministering to people with AIDS. He visited programs in London, Paris, Edinborough, Philadelphia, and San Francisco, returning not only with a lot of ideas but convinced that "churches need to respond to the AIDS crisis with a sense of urgency. There is a huge need for ministry that is going unmet."

In addition to establishing a "buddy" program (see St. Mark's p. 41), Christ Church helped create Hustead House, a residence and care facility for patients unable to remain at home. The church did some major fundraising to support the house and provided all the furnishings and many volunteers to help the staff. A Lutheran church joined the effort and now provides food and cooking for the house. There was some resistance from a few neighbors of Hustead House, located in a residential subdivision, but church support was unwavering. The church now pays for health insurance and medicine for AIDS patients staying at Hustead House.

The church also runs a support group for families and people working with AIDS patients. "The people that have worked with this issue really feel they are doing important work," he says. "The whole church is changed as a result. Members of the gay community that are a part of our church have become more active and have really responded with ministries of their own." Four other Episcopal churches in the Raleigh area are starting programs of their own, inspired by Christ Church's work.

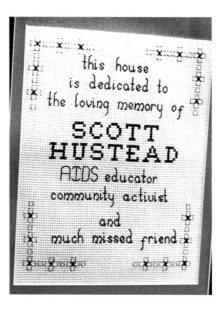

this house is dedicated to the loving memory of

SCOTT HUSTEAD

AIDS educator community activist and much missed friend

Legal Assistance, AIDS School Curriculums & More
The Catholic Church of St. Ann, Marietta, Georgia

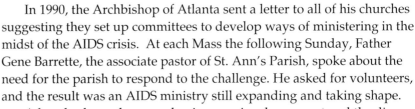

In 1990, the Archbishop of Atlanta sent a letter to all of his churches suggesting they set up committees to develop ways of ministering in the midst of the AIDS crisis. At each Mass the following Sunday, Father Gene Barrette, the associate pastor of St. Ann's Parish, spoke about the need for the parish to respond to the challenge. He asked for volunteers, and the result was an AIDS ministry still expanding and taking shape.

A hundred people, many having previously encountered the disease among friends or family, are participating. Many give care and support to AIDS patients and their families as "buddies," cooking, providing transportation, doing house or yard work, reaching out with whatever human or spiritual support is needed. A nun trained as a paralegal advises patients and families. The church provides some short-term financial support.

AIDS ministry members have also prepared and led AIDS education programs for high school and for middle school students. Presented yearly as part of the church's religious education program, the curriculums have now been used with over 2,000 children. As part of its effort to reach young people, a young married woman who is HIV positive wrote a letter that was sent to over 2000 youths in the parish. The teens have presented a play titled "AIDS: A Presence," writ-

St. Ann parish participates in a walk for AIDS.

ten and directed by a parishioner who is a college student. Every two months, Father Barrette and AIDS ministry members carry out a special AIDS liturgy created to support AIDS patients, their families and friends.

Overall, parish response has been positive. There have been a few raised eyebrows by some who have had difficulty separating the gay lifestyle of some AIDS victims from the disease itself. Father Barrette offers a reminder: "We're talking about sick people who are suffering. We don't question how they got it. That's not our concern."

The ministry is still growing, as more people realize the church is a place they can go for support without being judged, and more people whose lives have been affected by AIDS come forward wanting to help and be involved. "The ministry provides much needed care for AIDS patients," says Father Barrette, "but it also provides what can be a transforming life experience to those doing the care."

AIDS Care Teams Also Help Church to Grow
St. Mark's Episcopal Church, Corpus Cristi, Texas

"They have been mostly wonderful, educated, talented young men, dying horrendous deaths right in the prime of their lives." This is how St. Mark's Ann Rogers describes the people she has cared for as part of an AIDS Care Team. Outreach Chair Ed Parker states the goal of the program simply: "to add some comfort and dignity to their deaths."

St. Mark's got involved with AIDS ministry by asking Houston's AIDS Interfaith Council to come to the church and train two teams of ten to twelve people in caring for patients with advanced cases of AIDS. They learned about basic care — precautions to take in bathing and moving, etc. — and some basic nursing skills. They were told what to expect as the patients' conditions worsened, and they committed to give substantial time and effort to their team.

In their first two years, the teams of "buddies" helped 10 patients through the devastating process of dying. Team members shop, cook, run errands, clean, and provide a break for whoever is responsible for day-to-day care. "It is both a wonderful and a terribly taxing experience," says Ann. "At least one of us gets very attached to each patient. It's painful. It's easy to get burned out."

The church now hopes to add other hospice teams to care for people with other terminal diseases. Only six years old, this church was founded with a commitment to devote a good part of its budget to projects that were directly "hands-on" in helping others. The result is a church that has already grown to 550 members, with almost all involved in one of what Ann calls "the church's labors of love. Hands-on outreach efforts are a big part of why people increasingly choose to come here."

Robert Amayo (right) and Cynthia Rodriguez are volunteer "buddies" to Andy White (left) who is benefitting from St. Mark's outreach.

In Loving Memory and Celebration of
JEFF DICKSON

July 29, 1957 - November 28, 1991

The special memorial brochure Jeff Dickson's congregation prepared for his funeral service, shows their tenderness, understanding and love, particularly of sister choir member, Cindy Hammond.

Embracing an AIDS Victim in Their Congregation
Irvine United Church of Christ, Irvine, California

Increasingly, congregations find in their midst people who are dying of AIDS and who will need the same love as this church provided to choir member Jeff Dickson. As Irvine's pastor, Reverend Fred Plumer asserts, "We are not ministering to people with AIDS for some abstract or politically correct reasons, but because we have come to deeply care about and love people in our midst who are suffering."

The congregation kept Jeff fully a part of their faith community for as long as possible. They cared for him, touched him, kept him an active member of the choir as long as he was able. Through their love and care, they transformed what might have been a lonely death into an intimate time of sharing and deep meaning. Reverend Plumer recalls the day Jeff died, "As a breeze gently moved through the room, everyone present knew that they had truly experienced a spiritual phenomenon. They were all glad that God had shared Jeff with them."

Other Possibilities:

All Saints Episcopal Church, Pasadena, California, initiated and helped establish a big **AIDS treatment center** that operates separately from the church in a building of its own.

St. Mark's Episcopal Church, Corpus Christi, Texas, monthly **pays a hospital for doctor visits and medication** for 60 people who live on the streets. The hospital saves by treating people early as outpatients rather than admitting them as emergency "charity cases" coming in by ambulance.

St. Andrew's Episcopal Church, Barboursville, West Virginia, **recruited some doctors and nurses to volunteer in a clinic run in this tiny church** every Wednesday night. The church parlor is the waiting room, screening is done in the secretary's office, and the rector's study and a vesting area are the examining rooms. The 60 patients come from as far as 50 miles away. The church has gained some publicity and added new members!

Boston Avenue United Methodist Church, Tulsa, Oklahoma, **fields doctors and dentists to volunteer in an area clinic and travel abroad** to different communities. The church also **offers respite care** for people with dependents who need constant attention.

New ideas of your own?
Projects you like?
Jot them down on p. 97.

Young People
and Learning

Without a good education, a young person's choices for the future can be close to zero. Educational needs can include an affordable pre-school, an adult to help with homework, a school and neighborhood where you don't have to worry about being offered drugs or being shot, having a chance to go to college.

Congregations across the country are making alliances for education to address the full range of these needs. They adopt schools in formal relationships; run after-school programs; assure a college education for kids who otherwise wouldn't have the chance; turn simple day-care into an active pre-school, giving kids a chance to start out on the right foot.

Outside school, all children and young people need channels for growth, including opportunities to learn about the positive options adult life can hold for them. Encouraging young people to envision and participate in their own positive future is one of the most fundamental ways to make a difference — both in individual lives and in our society as a whole.

The backbone of many congregations' approach is being a mentor — a role model, an adult adviser, someone to confide in, a "door opener" to jobs or educational opportunities — and a friend. Many young people, often boys with absent fathers, urgently need the example of what it means to be a happy, productive adult, an example that someone in your congregation could give, along with advice and friendship — and love.

Story telling winners from the 5th and 4th grade with volunteer coach, Jane Levenson, from All Souls Unitarian Church, New York, New York (p. 50).

An After-School Partnership Between a Church and a Synagogue Blossoms and Grows Strong

Temple Emanu-El and Third Baptist Church, San Francisco, California

It's 2 p.m. Program Director Mary Vradelis is pouring juice into pitchers and making peanut butter and jelly sandwiches. Soon the children will come, and the tutors. And at one of the tables in the Third Baptist all purpose room there may even be a game of Monopoly, an ice-breaker for a student and his tutor meeting for the first time.

Lots of children can use one-on-one help with school work. The Back on Track after-school program is a partnership between Temple Emanu-El and Third Baptist Church to provide exactly that.

> *"I come out of here knowing that the time I spent was worthwhile."*
>
> **Alison Geballe, Tutor**

Over one hundred volunteers from the church, the temple and the community join forces to tutor, one-on-one, about a hundred children who want to do better in school. The program is supported by the temple, the church, and grants from the community. Program director Mary Vradelis happily reports dramatic improvements in work, participation and interest in school for most of the kids in Back on Track.

Lakeesha Gage and Alison Geballe have been figuring out homework together for years.

The volunteers and the children also gain invaluable experience crossing racial, social, and religious boundaries in ways that are mutually beneficial and enlightening.

Back on Track grew out of the resolve of the temple's Community Service Committee "to find opportunities for members of our temple to make a difference and be a reconciling force in our city," according to the temple's executive director, Gary Cohen. The program has also brought the two congregations closer. Besides contact during the after-school program, every year on the weekend of Dr. Martin Luther King's birthday the pastor and some congregants worship at the synagogue, and the church choir often sings. The next day, members of Emanu-El's congregation worship at the church, with the rabbi preaching.

Back on Track getting under way for the afternoon.

An After-School Alternative to the Streets
East San Diego United Presbyterian Church, San Diego, California

Solapkny Hian (left) and Jessica Gillette proudly display awards they've received.

"This is a neighborhood of crime, gangs, drugs and poverty. When kids get out of school each day, we want to give them a piece of another kind of life to hang on to. Maybe it will make all the difference later on," asserts a staffer about the after-school REACH program the church offers to elementary school children.

Back in 1983, this small multi-ethnic congregation responded to a need for language help and a safe, interesting, after-school environment by starting a low budget tutoring program with one volunteer and a bit of space. These days 35 kids are enrolled and 15 are on a waiting list.

The program remains absolutely free to the children and is supported by funds from the church, other congregations and the community. Volunteers from the church supplement the efforts of several staffers. Time is planned each day for homework, remedial math and English tutoring, reading aloud, a nutritional snack and recreational and educational games in the courtyard of the church, which lies right across the street from a park frequented by gang members. "We try, we really try," says program director John Palaylay.

A High Quality Pre-School - for $6 a Week
Bethany Presbyterian Church, Cleveland, Ohio

Bethany is a small inner city church whose neighborhood has high unemployment. Many transient people live in residence hotels. Alcoholism, drug use and domestic violence are common.

In this setting, the pre-school this church runs aims to "strengthen learning skills, foster positive self-image, develop social skills, teach peacemaking skills, and work with parents."

The pre-school operates half days, three days a week, providing an excellent program for about 35 families a year. Each half day costs the family just $2!

Total school operating costs come to about $30,000. Half comes from the Presbytery and from government block grants through the West Side Ecumenical Ministry which was started by Bethany and other neighborhood churches in 1966. Bethany, other churches, foundations, women's groups, and fundraisers supply most of the rest. Only about $4,500 comes from the $2 fees.

Quality is as important as making sure the program is offered at very low cost. There's a dedicated staff of a director, two teachers, and a classroom aide. An important aspect of the pre-school is working with families on parenting skills and family cooperation, and affirming the parents so they can affirm their children.

A teacher works with children at Bethany Presbyterian Church's low cost pre-school program.

A City and a Suburban Church Jointly Adopt a School

Second Grace United Methodist Church, Detroit, Michigan and
First United Methodist Church, Northville, Michigan

Concern for children in a troubled school system and a need to make a place for itself in a new neighborhood came together for Second Grace Unite methodist Church when it formed a partnership with First United Methodist Church and adopted a school.

A few years ago, Second Grace's former pastor attended a Detroit Board of Education meeting where the idea that local churches might "adopt" a neighborhood school was presented. Feeling that doing the job well might be a task beyond their resources, Second Grace proposed a partnership with a larger suburban church to adopt Dixon Elementary School near Second Grace. First UMC accepted the partnership proposal, happy for an opportunity to get involved with the city and be an agent for positive change. The relationship is a formal one, with a written commitment agreement proudly displayed for all church members to see.

The backbone of the partnership is the mentoring program. People from both churches sign up for a minimum of one year with a child. They commit to being a role model and spending at least one hour each week with the child, helping with homework and going on outings. Both churches aim for 10% of their members serving as mentors.

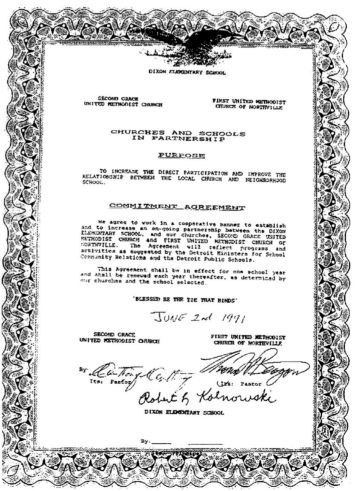

Volunteers from the churches go into the school daily to read stories and help out in classrooms. There is a fall clean-up and work day when church people do painting, landscaping, cleaning and other work for the school. Second Grace put on a spring awards banquet for school staff, parents and children, giving prizes for academic achievement, citizenship, and attendance. A summer picnic is held at the Northville church, and overall, as current pastor of Second Grace, Reverend Emmanuel Bailey observes, the relationship continues to grow in strength.

Making College Possible: An Alliance between a Church, a School and a College
Scott Memorial United Methodist Church, Detroit, Michigan

A high school and a college have joined forces to create a new kind of education and a new future for some young people in Detroit. The catalyst and the partner that makes it work is a church.

A few years ago when he was appointed to Scott Memorial UMC, former pastor, Dr. Anthony Shipley, was already on the board of directors of Adrian College. Adrian is a small, liberal arts college outside Detroit and has been named by *U.S. News and World Report* as one of America's best colleges.

Adrian was working to increase its minority enrollment, and the church was looking for ways to make a difference in a community where drugs, drop-out rates, and unemployment among young African-Americans are persistent problems.

Colin Kelley (left) is on his way to college thanks to the ASPIRES program which Dr. Shipley (right) helped start.

Dr. Shipley had the idea of starting a collaboration of the church, the college and Mackenzie high school, which is right across the street from the church. MacKenzie's principal took Dr. Shipley quite seriously when he showed up in his office with the president of Adrian College ready to make a commitment. The three set things in motion; the result is the ASPIRES program.

Three Adrian professors worked with high school teachers in math, science, and English to redesign the curriculum. Thirty students in each class year were selected for a special program that would guarantee admission to Adrian.

Scott UMC created a tutoring program in their community center, employing board-certified teachers to work with young people twice a week. A mentoring program was set up, giving each student a back-up family for support and encouragement. Many Detroit dignitaries got involved as mentors.

The ASPIRES program now reaches back to the junior high level. This year, 30 Mckenzie High graduates are expected to be enrolled at Adrian, 12 sophomores and 18 freshman, each of whom will receive substantial financial support that doesn't have to be repaid if they perform well at Adrian.

The church and its community center now find themselves at the center of this exciting collaboration. Under a new minister, Dr. Andrew Allie, the congregation continues in its enthusiastic support.

Scott UMC and, across the street, MacKenzie High School.

One to One Makes All the Difference
Zion Baptist Church, Philadelphia, Pennsylvania

They're clearly close. Cyrus, the mentor; Anthony, the 5th grader. It's Sunday afternoon. As they drive and then walk around Philadelphia, showing a visitor the sights, they talk to each other in low, comfortable voices. They don't have to say much because they know each other well.

At times Anthony will touch Cyrus, putting his hand on Cyrus's shoulder as they walk along, as if to gently reassure himself that Cyrus is there and is going to stay there. Then there's a burst of energy, each trying to out-do the other, jumping up on a wall.

This is what it's all about: a real relationship between a youngster and a caring adult of the same sex. Not a replacement for a parent, but another adult who can be a friend and role model, for at least one whole year of a young person's life.

Cyrus, a businessman, and Anthony, who lives in a Presbyterian boys' home near the city, are one of 20 child/mentor pairs in Zion Baptist's One to One program. Each adult makes a commitment to spend at least two hours a month in two face-to-face contacts with the youngster. Sometimes there are group outings, or the pairs decide to do things on their own. Costs come out of the mentor's pocket.

Zion also requires the mentor make at least two other contacts each month, by phone or letter, so at minimum it works out to be a once-a-week commitment for the year. But clearly many of the rela-

tionships grow deep and will last well beyond the first year.

Zion's mentoring program is modeled on the nationwide One to One program (see *Resources*) that started in 1991. The national organization provides training for coordinators of local programs, who in turn train the mentors. The local programs decide how they will recruit youngsters.

Lynda Downes is a member of Zion Baptist's congregation and the area mentoring director for a network of Philadelphia churches involved in mentoring. Her regular job is with United Way which is in partnership with One to One in Philadelphia. "The kids really, really love it," says Ms. Downes.

On the drive back to the boys' home, Anthony falls asleep. Cyrus notices and turns the stereo down.

Anthony (the youngster) and Cyrus taking advantage of a warm spring Philadelphia day to see some sights and spend time together.

The Focus is Children:
Opening Doors and Creating Fun
Unitarian Church of All Souls, New York, New York

The chess workshop at Eleanor Roosevelt is a hotbed of activity.

Mary Ella Holst (All Souls) and Reverend Leroy Ricksy (Resurrection) check out the new portable classroom for Booker T. Washington Center.

Doing homework at Booker T.

According to the church's Bond of Union, a central part of the life of All Souls Church is "the service of all." That phrase is taken seriously in this 1000-member church, where over 500 people are actively engaged as volunteers in social ministries. "We emphasize deeds, not creeds, in this church," says Senior Minister Forrester Church, who describes the congregation as a community of service.

Working with children, and on children's issues, is a major part of this service. There's a Children's Task Force that shapes most of the programs. Says Jeanne North, a former chair of the task force: "Our mission is to serve children at risk because of poverty, home circumstances, the environment in which they live. We're trying to give them some other experiences, because it's so hard to get into the system when you're out of the system. It's hard to find that door in."

One open door is the Booker T. Washington Learning Center in East Harlem, which All Souls set up in partnership with their sister church, Church of the Resurrection, United Church of Christ. Housed in Resurrection's basement, Booker T. has a pre-school, an after-school tutoring program, and a summer program.

"I think we're seen as partners in this community . . . we're trying to give a boost to partnerships."

Donna Cassetta,

All Souls Volunteer

The newest addition to the center is the first of three portable classrooms, made possible through All Souls' fundraising efforts and a grant from the Calder Foundation, 42nd Street Development Corporation and other groups. It's across the street and is allowing Booker T. to expand and accept more children. At the urging of All Souls and the Urban Center, the city is also helping to create a small park on the lot.

All Souls raised the funds for Booker T. and also supplied the computers, volunteers for the tutoring program, and teachers. But the idea originated with someone from the community. "This is Melissa's idea," says Mary-Ella Holst, All Souls' lead person for Booker T. "She goes to the Church of the Resurrection, she was raised in that housing project, she played in that field as a little girl. One day Melissa said, 'We ought to get a portable classroom module'. She persisted, everyone got enthused, and it happened. People have good ideas about their own lives."

Adding fun and enrichment into the public school day is another focus for All Souls. With support from the Franklin and Eleanor Roosevelt Foundation, the church has adopted the Eleanor Roosevelt Elementary School (PS 151). Donna Cassetta, All Souls' volunteer coordinator for the school, explains: "They're lacking some of the most fun things you get from school, like a school play, learning an instrument, drawing .. we want to give them what every child deserves, a well-rounded experience in school."

Volunteers work with the school's PTA to provide enrichment projects. They work as tutors in classrooms, in the school library and as sponsors for special events. The church hires a professional children's theater director who with many volunteers has worked with a large number of children to create the "Warp 'N' Woof" children's theater. Their first production was "Rappin' Romeo."

Volunteer with his breakfast club friend, getting off to a good start.

Then there's the Breakfast Club. As Donna explains, "It was the principal's idea, that each adult has one child they come in and see before school so each starts the day right and has one person caring about them because they don't have that kind of attention at home. There are a lot of single people who could do that."

She says that all the work with the school is seen as "a cooperative effort, and that's the spirit the principal approaches it in; everyone, including the teachers, are part of the effort."

A third All Souls program involving children is a number of Scout troops: boys, girls, and cubs. The Boy Scouts was started after an All Souls member had been working with some children living in one of New York's welfare hotels.

Boy Scouts learn CPR with an All Souls volunteer.

The Boy Scouts initially met at another Unitarian church, several blocks from the hotel. According to Jeanne, "it was a scary exercise, just picking up the boys and taking them back and forth." Two years later the hotel closed, but the troop continues, now meeting at a center on East 109th Street in Harlem. Some of the original boys still attend!

Broadening opportunities for kids also has an impact on their families and their community. As Mary-Ella says, "The kids can inspire their parents!"

In summing up the church's work with children, Mary-Ella observes: "These kids are full of hope, and what's religion about if it's not about hope?"

Warp & Woof theatre in rehearsal.

Other Possibilities:

Metropolitan Baptist Church, Pensacola, Florida, has an extremely successful Extended Arms **program for youth offenders** sentenced to the program when they appear before a judge for a minor crime. Three days a week, juvenile first and second offenders gather at the church for counseling on alcohol, drugs or anger; for emotional or family counseling; and for tutoring in a program coordinated with their teachers.

Alta Vista Christian Church, Kansas City, Missouri became a partner in an **alternative high school program** for kids with problems. Initially set up in the church using its classrooms and other facilities, the school was run in cooperation with a social service agency and has since been moved to its own building.

Church of the Resurrection, Omaha, Nebraska drew together a group of parents and a group of artists to plan **an enrichment program** to reach inner city kids with positive, alternative values. In Soul Fire, kids from 5th grade on up meet for eight sessions on Saturday mornings to develop basic skills in the arts and learn about their black cultural heritage, working with a poet, a painter, a musician, a dancer, and a dramatist. Simultaneously, parents attend a program on the traditions and values of the African-American family.

New ideas of your own?
Projects you like?
Jot them down on p. 97.

Jobs and Income

JOBS AND INCOME

Having a job, being able to "bring home the bacon," is fundamental to stability and progress. For many, there either is no work or there is limited access to work. Access to jobs can be crippled by not speaking English, by illiteracy, by lack of training or simply by lack of experience with the working world. Even well qualified people may be out of work in this era of down-sizing. Congregations can be a channel for increasing people's access to jobs.

At work in the business incubator (see story p. 58).

Congregations can also help create jobs, by helping existing businesses to grow and new ones to develop. Starting a business is a great way to find work, and in time the business can provide jobs for still others. Start-up costs can be the killer; a business incubator and some expert advice from your members can be a solution.

Even with space and advice, businesses need capital. By creating or investing in institutions which make loans in areas where capital is in short supply, you can directly promote business development, create jobs, and help a community's economy.

Finally, there are ways to boost people's income if they are stuck in low-paying jobs or lack direct access to markets for their products.

Employment Watch Meets Job Seekers' Needs
St. Timothy's Roman Catholic Church, Norwood, Massachusetts

For people looking for jobs, and others who feel their jobs are in jeopardy, St. Timothy's offers Employment Watch. It's a structured support program for members of St. Timothy's and their friends.

As many as 35 people attend the sessions, which are led by a human services professional from the congregation. Members of the group share details of their own job hunting efforts and receive advice, support and help from the others. Guest professionals come in occasionally to teach interviewing, networking and resume writing skills. Members also network with each other.

The sessions are a good blend of practical advice, mutual support, and humor. Meetings open with a prayer and end with "Next Steps." This is an action-oriented program — and it gets results!

Vern Ludwig (center), the group's leader, is the catalyst for some networking.

A Collection Plate Full of Business Cards
St. Paul's Episcopal Church, Alexandria, Virginia

To address rising unemployment in this mostly white-collar congregation, Rector Geoffrey Hoare had the idea of using the natural network of the church more fully. On various Sunday mornings, people were asked to put their business cards into the offering plates if they were willing to help those looking for work.

In short order, a "network list" was created of people offering resources, contacts, suggestions, phones and office space, informational interviews, or job possibilities. This list became a huge help to those in the parish's employment support group.

Area Jobs Listing Becomes Invaluable Resource
Temple Beth Am, Merrick, New York

In the heart of the recession, Rabbi Ron Brown was trying to help out-of-work congregation members to find jobs. He had an idea: expand his own temple's network for the benefit of his congregation and oth-

CODE	PROFESSION	EXPERIENCE/DESCRIPTION	YRS WORK EXP	EDUCATION
234	Sales	Operations/Production Mgr/Administrator	15	BA
235	Teacher	Jewish/Secular Education/Legal Proofreader	3	BA
236	Electronics Engineer	Design & Development-- Electrical Design Equip	15	BS

ers. Through the New York Board of Rabbis, a thousand rabbis in the greater New York area were sent a letter to read to their congregations on Yom Kippur. People needing jobs were asked to give their resumes to their rabbi, people with jobs to offer would supply job descriptions.

The rabbis sent those items to the Board; Temple Beth Am's Brotherhood was then given the resumes and job descriptions to summarize. Anonymity was preserved: job seekers were given code numbers assigned by the Board. The resulting listings were distributed to all participating synagogues. A call to the Board puts job seekers and jobs together. Updates of the listings are sent out on a regular basis.

"It's not an original idea. It's the kind of thing that congregations have been doing for generations. It's just on a scale large enough to be of realistic help in our day."

Rabbi Ron Brown

Helping Eradicate Illiteracy in the Community, Even in Prison
Southminster Presbyterian Church, Dayton, Ohio

Volunteer tutor signs in to Dayton correctional to meet the inmate he tutors in literacy.

Southminster Presbyterian, located in a suburban area of Dayton, was looking for a more effective way to make a difference in the city. Wanting to get past the "band-aid" approach and take on some of the causes of urban poverty, the church focused on literacy.

Dayton's Literacy Council didn't believe that a program could work from the suburbs, and eventually Southminster had to pay trainers to come to the church and train volunteers. However, the Literacy Council was stunned by the turnout of volunteers, and then by the number of people who took advantage of tutoring.

Currently, many volunteers serve over a hundred students. Two volunteers have taken the

"Many of our own people did not believe this could be done from the suburbs, but we now feel like we are truly part of the city."

Reverend Robert Smith

program into the county prison. Reverend Robert Smith feels the whole church's life has been revitalized by people's direct relationships with the people they are trying to help.

Summer Jobs and Self-Esteem for At-Risk Young People
Advent Lutheran Church, Boca Raton, Florida

"Our community, like most, is filled with young people who are unemployed or underemployed because they were never able to finish high school," says Reverend Ron Dingle. "We wanted to take some of the kids who are most at risk for problems or for dropping out of school and give them another direction."

Advent Lutheran's LEAD program was the result. The church agreed to employ 18 young people for five dollars an hour for 30 hours a week during the summer. The work lasted for six hours each day, after which all of the kids

were gathered for educational sessions, called the "growth hour." Here they discussed self-esteem, communication, setting goals, discipline and leadership.

Few kids had any work experience at all and struggled with the regimen, but not a single one dropped out. "What we saw come out of the program was more than worth the relatively small monetary investment that the church made," says Reverend Dingle.

Young people in the LEAD program paint and do yard and fix-up work for the church and area residents. The people who hire LEAD kids pay $7/hour; the kids earn $5 and the difference goes to running the program.

A Unique Restaurant that Trains People

First Trinity Lutheran Church, Washington, D.C.

The busy restaurant in the Capitol district of Washington, D.C. doesn't look unusual, but it's part of an extraordinary effort by the 200-family First Trinity Lutheran Church, just a block away. "It gives you a chance to get back what you had before and gives you a little bit more," says a trainee about the program that has helped him put the pieces of his life back together after years of homelessness and substance abuse.

Since 1969, First Trinity has ministered to the poor and homeless of central Washington through Community Family Life Services (CFLS), a social service agency created by First Trinity but now supported by many churches. In 1986 two apartment buildings on the next block were slated to be replaced by a commercial building. The church formed a separate non-profit corporation that bought the buildings and transformed them into Trinity Arms, transitional housing.

One day, as CFLS Director (and First Trinity's Associate Pastor) Reverend Tom Knoll was trying to envision ways to use Trinity Arms' basement to advantage, it occurred to him that there were very few restaurants in the immediate area but a lot of workers looking for lunch. A restaurant would be labor-intensive and could provide temporary jobs for formerly homeless people and training for jobs in the job market.

Today that basement is "3rd & Eats" (the name taken from the address of 3rd and E Streets), a self-service deli serving a substantial breakfast and lunchtime crowd. As one patron put it, "You get a good lunch at a fair price and do some good besides."

Eight trainees help three full-time professional workers, hired by CFLS to run the restaurant and prepare the food. The trainees, some of whom live in apartments upstairs, earn $45 a week and must adhere to the chef's rules. After they have enough experience, they get help finding regular jobs.

CFLS used a $400,000 low-interest loan from the Lutheran Church, Missouri Synod, to do the renovations. So far, 3rd 'n Eats has been a great success and has made the loan payments on time. But the unanticipated need to pay the $2,300-per-trainee training costs is delaying the point at which the restaurant will be profitable. As Mary Lou Tietz, associate director says, "If individual churches

On the job at lunch hour, the head chef (left), coordinator Joe Gemmell (middle) and trainee Daryl Crittendon.

could provide that kind of support, it would really help." Eventually, all profits will go to the church's programs for the homeless.

Mary Lou drops in daily to help solve problems. "It's a wonderful training opportunity....and I feel very good about the respect we have for the trainees: they're doing a big service for us, and we hope that in turn we're doing a big service for them, and we are committed to getting them employed."

A Business Incubator and a
69%-for-Outreach Budget
Community Baptist Church, Milwaukee, Wisconsin

"It's better to provide jobs and a way out of a troubled economic situation than it is to have give-away programs. The church must not only preach the word, but teach people how they can have a more abundant life." William Lock reflects on his motivation as Vice President of Community Enterprises of Greater Milwaukee (CEGM), an economic development center started and run by Community Baptist Church.

People working at one of the small businesses housed in the Community Enterprises of Greater Milwaukee business incubator building.

"There's a mutual need for us to be involved with business. It not only helps the individual, it supports the community at large."

Reverend Roy Nabors

Housed in an old warehouse donated by a local businessman, this "Business Incubator" now houses five small businesses that employ 45 people. Another hundred people are employed by businesses that have graduated from the program. CEGM was funded the first two years by the church, with volunteers doing most of the warehouse renovations. The incubator provides low-rent space and management assistance to minority owned start-up companies.

Community Baptist is in an area of Milwaukee devastated by plant closings and in a state of "absolute depression." Chairman James Jones says: "If people around here can't make it, we can't make it. Somewhere along the line, we have to show people that there is help and there is hope. Until we do that we're all going to have a problem, I don't care where we live."

The incubator provides that help and hope. Any individual who has a business idea can get advice and training.

Community Baptist has 13 different community outreach ministries, which take up 69% of its income. They run three different day-care programs for children of low-income families and an infant care center for babies with special problems. These centers employ 22 people who might not otherwise have found work. The church also serves a daily breakfast that serves 10,000 meals a year.

All this work reflects the commitment the congregation made when established in 1977. "We want to live our incarnational theology," says Reverend Nabors, "and we're willing to try anything that helps people toward a fuller life."

Helping Create a Minority-Owned Bank with a Focus on Economic Development
Tenth Memorial Baptist Church, Philadelphia, Pennsylvania

"We needed to find a way to use the resources of the African-American community to rebuild and recharge that community." This is how Reverend William B. Moore talks about the reason for creating a minority-owned bank in Philadelphia. "Technically, we haven't had 'redlining' in our neighborhoods, but there have been very limited resources for investment in minority businesses or for loans to minority individuals with mixed credit histories. So we wanted to create a financial institution that was about that very thing."

In the mid-eighties, when interstate banking regulations changed, a New Jersey bank was selling its single branch in Philadelphia. Seeing this as an opportunity not to be missed, the African-American community and key black churches such as Tenth Baptist decided to try to buy and capitalize the bank. They needed $1.2 million to do it.

Their efforts at raising the money within the required time failed. They didn't give up, though, and when the opportunity was still there a year later, they redoubled their efforts. By this time, in a more difficult economic climate and with tougher state regulators, they needed a total of $5 million in investments.

A new board of directors was organized, and many of the city's leading minority citizens were asked to be members. The whole range of Philadelphia's black religious community became involved. A Black Bank Sunday was held in most minority churches. Investments were solicited and churches made deposit commitments. Eventually, over $4 million dollars in investments was raised from within the African-American community in $500 and $1000 shares. Another $2 million was invested by other banking institutions. Thus, the first minority-owned, full service bank in Philadelphia was chartered.

Reverend Moore, pastor of Tenth Memorial, one of the key churches supporting the creation of the bank and currently a member of its board, proudly displays the plaque celebrating United Bank's opening.

The bank plans to make a profit for its investors, but its mission is to do that by investing in economic development in minority communities. "The bank has an educational mission as well. We will do programs to teach people about managing money, applying for loans, and understanding how the financial system works," says Reverend Moore. The deposit base is also becoming more metropolitan, individuals and churches such as suburban Central Baptist Church seeing United Bank as a vehicle for making their money help in the inner city.

Veteran Philadelphia banker and United Bank's CEO, Dr. Emma Chappell, was a leading force in creating the bank. She is shown here with a unique system she introduced in Philadelphia which allows people to do paper work comfortably while they wait in line.

A Place to Grow Their Own

Our Redeemer Lutheran Church, Livingston, California

A farmer and his daughter head out to the site.

Reverend Ruth (center) discussing planting with some of the farmers.

A farmer carries irrigation pipes to the site for installation.

"This is really a miracle!" said Reverend Bill Ruth, about seven acres of San Joaquin Valley farmland about to be planted.

The land was a valuable building lot — across the street from the large house of one of the wine-making Gallo brothers. Instead, a member of Reverend Ruth's congregation donated it, to be worked and managed by migrant farm workers, landless year-round farm workers, and people living in apartments in the small town of Livingston, about 100 miles southeast of San Francisco.

The "miracle" is also that the land had lain fallow, with no chemicals used for seven years, so produce raised on it can be certified as organic, according to California law. The dollar yield is much higher for organically raised vegetables, such as fancy white and orange tomatoes much sought after by gourmet restaurants. Crop yield can be increased dramatically, by "French intensive farming," which produces vigorous plants that you grow close together.

This is not just a story about successful, high-yield farming. It's also a tale of persistence and faith on the part of "Pastor Bill", with a touch of the story of the three — really four — bears.

Livingston has a community of farm workers year round, and migrant workers from spring to fall. Between October and May, there is no farm work at all. When there is work, wages are very low and sometimes hard to collect. A mattress on the floor can cost $28 a night! Clearly, the workers badly needed something to boost their incomes.

Reverend Ruth and Glen Anderson, who chairs the California Alliance of Family Farmers (CAFF), decided to create a community farm where workers could raise food for themselves and also have something to sell. Reverend Ruth began the search for land, working closely with Rufino Dominguez, leader of the migrant workers from Oaxaca, Mexico. An organizer, Dominguez heads the Organization of Oppressed and Exploited People, helping with immigration and labor problems.

Here is where the four bears come in. The first piece of land, made available by two members of CAFF was too far away, a two-mile walk to weed and water the plants. The second parcel, just a mile out of town, donated by a couple in the congregation, was alternately too wet or too dry. A third piece was close in, but too expensive to insure.

The fourth piece, however, was just right! "It looks like all our ducks are in a row this time," said Reverend Ruth, "and we're going to be involving high school kids, farm workers, apartment dwellers —— it's really going to be a community farm. Our big organizational meeting is coming, when we'll be going to elect a board of directors, an advisory person, a chair person, and from there the leadership will plan out the plots and distribute the land as people sign up."

The "Seeds of Hope,"
A Unique Farm and City Program
Washington Street United Methodist Church, Columbia, South Carolina

1986 was a catastrophic drought year in South Carolina. In response, Washington Street UMC held an adult education Lenten study of hunger and the farm crisis. Inspired to find out more, mission chair Donna Bryan took a trip to a Methodist project that works with some of the state's poorest farmers in the Sea Islands of Charleston County, South Carolina. Donna met a group of farmers who shared their problems and frustrations with her. Over and over again, they identified a reliable market as their greatest need. Big packing companies and grocery chains bought inconsistently and offered very low prices. The farmers were barely hanging on. Ms. Bryan decided that the church could create a reliable market and eliminate the middleman.

Under her leadership, the church worked that summer with a half-dozen farmers to create a farmers market in the church parking lot on Saturdays. They called it Seeds of Hope. When the harvest started to come in, the farmers loaded their produce and drove 150 miles to the church. The church advertised the market and it thrived. Church volunteers got first crack at the fresh food, and the farmers got the a market for their products that made the difference between desperate poverty and a decent living.

A South Carolina farmer's daughter with a bag of corn.

Both the people buying and those selling have been encouraged to talk and interact with each other as a way to help urban people understand more about rural life and problems and vice versa. The farmers, selling their goods in urban areas, were moved by the sight of poor and homeless people hanging around some of the market sites. They began donating food left over from market days to area shelters and food banks.

Seeds of Hope now even ships to New York City, supplying produce not provided by northern farmers but needed in making traditional African-American dishes that originated in the rural south. The food goes to a farmers market in Harlem and to one in Brooklyn run by an African-American church in its Bedford-Stuyvesant parking lot.

In Washington Street's parking lot on a busy market day.

One church's "small idea" has blossomed into an ecumenical and interfaith program involving 16 Columbia churches and synagogues benefitting literally thousands of people, with very little expense to anyone. "And people from different worlds are coming together and gaining new understanding," says Ms. Bryan, " an understanding, especially, about their wonderful interdependence."

Other Possibilities:

Community loan funds (see BCLF story, p. 73, and *Resources* section) can be a way for your congregation to invest to help businesses get started, since many funds provide business loans as well as financial support for housing.

KAM Isaiah Israel, Chicago, Illinois, has created **"dedicated" bank accounts** so its members' money and congregational funds can help "leverage" the bank in making higher risk loans.

Irvine United Church of Christ, Irvine, California, took a **public stand supporting legislation that would outlaw job discrimination based on sexual preference**.

St. Jules Catholic Church, Lafayette, Louisiana, **established a credit union which lends money to people who don't need or won't accept charity.** The union has assets of over $4 million, makes hundreds of loans each year, and has only one full-time employee. The rest of the work is carried on by volunteers.

New ideas of your own?
Projects you like?
Jot them down on p. 97.

Homes and Neighborhoods

Throughout the country there is a great need for affordable housing and neighborhood renewal. Having a decent house in a safe and stable neighborhood has a powerful impact on people's lives. It's the base from which to find and keep a job, the place to raise children, and the reality that makes those children believe that they can have a place called home when they grow up.

Barnraising is an old American tradition. Many congregations have used similar cooperative building efforts to build houses for low income people. Other housing projects include helping people fix up their homes (a great short term project!), major rehabilitation, and transitional housing and services for people moving out of homelessness. A congregation can also help finance affordable housing by investing in it, individually or collectively.

Focusing on *all* the needs of the community, not just the physical ones, is crucial for neighborhood renewal. Many communities need to be freed from drugs and crime. Others would benefit from a community center, where people can gather in a safe, energized place. And rapidly diversifying neighborhoods need a way for people to connect and find common ground.

Each year, as part of their confirmation class training in what it means to serve, teens from Church of the Risen Savior in Albuquerque, New Mexico, help build a Habitat house on a lot the church has bought.

Celebrating a Centennial by Building a Habitat for Humanity House
First Friends Meeting, Greensboro, North Carolina

First Friends Meeting, a Quaker congregation, had a centennial year in 1991. Instead of observing that anniversary in one of the traditional ways, they decided to celebrate by giving expression to the values that gave meaning to those first hundred years — by building a Habitat for Humanity house, raising $40,000 and supplying virtually all the labor.

"I have never seen a project of any kind so wholeheartedly and unequivocally endorsed by everyone." said Reverend Stevens. As thousands of congregations across the country have found, Habitat home building projects can provide not only badly needed low income housing, but also deeply meaningful direct involvement for a congregation. Habitat for Humanity (see *Resources* section) through local affiliates helps with organization, a lot to build on, foundation work, materials and no-interest financing to the homeowners.

For First Friends, the project became the very center of the church's life. Each day started with meditation and worship. Reflections on the work became the theme of every Sunday service. "The building itself," said Reverend Stevens, "was a worship experience."

The floor was laid by noon. The workers danced together on it, singing their theme song, "Doing It For Love." The new homeowner, putting in her own sweat equity, danced along with them. The home was completed in just three weeks, with 178 people involved.

Church, Synagogue Join Forces to Build a Home
Holy Trinity Lutheran Church, Congregation B'Nai Torah, Seattle, Washington

It's a standard, 1,050 foot Habitat house. But there's nothing "standard" about the way it was built—by a church and a synagogue which jointly undertook the project and paid all the construction costs.

The idea came with Reverend Woody Carlson when he moved to Holy Trinity as Associate Pastor. Making it a joint project happened quickly. Says Reverend Carlson, "We had some connections with the temple and we thought, wouldn't it be great ... I called Jim Morel, B'nai Torah's rabbi, and he jumped at it." The timing was perfect: B'nai Torah's Social Action Committee was looking for a hands-on housing project. There was also a "sparkplug" in each congregation: Marta Hurwitz from the temple and Beth Boylan from the church.

Habitat of Seattle linked the congregations with the Saephan family (originally from Laos), who would work the required 500 hours on the house.

For the two congregations, the hours together on the job, the joint auction and other fundraising, the planning meetings and events were both fun and productive, and brought them much closer. It took the Saephan family out of a dangerous neighborhood into a bright new home they will own, paying it off with an interest-free, 20-year loan from Habitat for Humanity.

from left: Cheng and Kao Saephan (family), Christine Lukas and Paige Kelso (Holy Trinity), and Josh Rosenstein (B'nai Torah) work together putting up siding.

Fixing Up Homes, and a Unique Self-Help Program
First Church of Mission, Mission, Texas

"We've touched a lot of people and we've changed a lot of lives," says Betty Bundy, director of the Mission Service Project, "and that's what it's all about." Mission is located on the Rio Grande river where there are large settlements of Mexican-Americans who are field workers. Most of the housing in their settlements, called colonias, is makeshift at best. At Ms. Bundy's urging the church's Outreach Board allocated $3,000 to set up a program to renovate housing in the colonias.

The church sent out appeals to all the Methodist churches in its district, asking for volunteers, especially youth groups. They came, worked eight hours a day and slept on the floor of the church. People from Mission provided meals. "The young people are tremendous workers," Ms. Bundy says. "We don't give them easy tasks. They've rebuilt whole houses."

Fixing up houses in the colonias around Mission, Texas.

Now, after 12 years, volunteer groups from all over the Southwest are still coming—hundreds a year, young and old. Other churches in the area have joined the effort and provide food for workers and places to stay. The program raises $50,000 yearly, mostly in donations from churches and congregations in the Rio Grande Valley.

Mission has also branched out into self-help housing, using a foundation grant, in a project combining housing construction, employment training, and leadership development for poor families. Each year 15 families are selected, mostly Mexican-American field workers, to be part of the 46-week program. Under the tutelage of a master carpenter and plumber, the heads of the households (men or women) learn the skills necessary to build houses. Working together as a construction crew, they build homes for each other, 15 in all. Nothing is subcontracted; the workers do every part of the job. Houses are constructed on one central site and then moved to small pieces of land owned by the families.

People in the colonias who get involved with First Church of Mission's self-help program build their own houses, acquiring both job skills and a home.

One woman proudly working on the house that would soon be hers reported that six months earlier she hadn't even known how to use a hammer. Now she does carpentry, plumbing, electrical work, even a little cabinet making. Each worker learns something about each part of the construction process, but most strive to develop a specialty that will help them get a job when the program ends.

Participants spend two hours a week learning English or math, and two hours in classes on self-sufficiency training, parenting skills, home management and community leadership. "We want these people to go back to their communities as leaders and examples that can have an impact on their neighborhoods," says Ms. Bundy.

Workers earn minimum wage during construction and then take out a loan through the Federal Home Loan Bank subsidy program to buy their homes. The cost of the three-bedroom homes is around $10,000, and the payments usually under $100 a month.

The Church & Temple Corporation
Renovates Skid Row Housing

All Saints Episcopal Church, Pasadena California, and
Leo Baeck Temple, Los Angeles, California

"We came from completely different faith perspectives," says Rabbi Sandy Ragins of the Leo Baeck Temple, "but in our work together for others, the differences dissolved away. Our common vision, formed out of individual roots, held us together." Rabbi Ragins is reflecting the experience of working with All Saints Episcopal Church to renovate hotels in the "skid row" area of Los Angeles.

Church-synagogue cooperation goes back many years—to the late 1960s, when they joined in founding the Interfaith Center to Reverse the Arms Race. Several years ago, with the Center's work slowing, the congregations found another reason to work together.

Church & Temple president, Steve Moses of Leo Baeck, in front of some of the housing being renovated.

Much of the housing used by the poorest residents of this area is provided through "SRO's" (Single Resident Occupancy units). Most of these derelict hotels were scheduled for demolition; their low-income tenants would likely end up homeless.

Responding to this crisis, Leo Baeck and All Saints, 25 miles away in Pasadena, formed a non-profit housing alliance called the Church & Temple Corporation. Joining with the Skid Row Housing Trust, they purchased three derelict buildings on one of the worst blocks in the neighborhood. The first building was renamed Genesis to celebrate the project's beginning.

They obtained money from a variety of sources. A considerable amount of sweat equity was also involved. Members of both congregations contributed a huge amount of time, but each congregation only needed to provide $10,000 to the multi-million dollar project. Despite some rough financial moments, over 90 housing units were completed.

Working on a room at the Genesis.

The congregations' involvement didn't end there. They tried to establish an ongoing relationship with the people living in the buildings. A dentist from the temple offered free dental care to tenants, and a recovering alcoholic started an Alcoholics Anonymous group.

The project has created momentum beyond itself. At the urging of the two congregations, the Episcopal Bishop of the Los Angeles Diocese and the head of the Federation of Reform Temples called a joint meeting of representatives of area congregations to create other church-temple partnerships. Two other partnerships are already pursuing projects based on this model.

An Alternative to Institutional Living for the Handicapped

Hillsboro Presbyterian Church, Hillsboro, Tennessee

Several years ago, the Hillsboro church entered into a partnership with Progress Inc., an agency that creates and runs group school program for handicapped adults that is attended by up to 35 people from other group homes in the area. The volunteers who staff

(from left to right) Virgie Miller, Reverend Nancy McCurley, Diane Hunter, and Ron Turner coming back from a trip.

"We wanted to provide an example of a real alternative to institutional living, where a community takes responsibility for its members. They are part of us, and it is a gift of God to have them among us."

Associate Pastor Nancy McCurley

Faith house is in a lovely setting right on the church's property.

homes for the mentally and physically handicapped. They undertook the substantial renovation of a house on the church grounds to turn into their own pilot home. Several thousand dollars were raised, and a large crew of volunteers set out to turn a derelict building into a real home for eight handicapped adults. Church people did construction work, painted, wallpapered, and furnished the house. They dubbed it Faith House—after a senior member of the church named Faith.

Some of the eight current residents of the house are developmentally disabled, some are severely physically handicapped, but all have found a home at Hillsboro. There is a Sunday

the Sunday school class consider it the high point of their week. There is a lot of singing and hugging going on. "The love in that room just amazes me every week," says teacher Scott Brunette. Most of the handicapped people attend worship; some serve on committees; many are part of a Sunday lunch program along with others in the congregation. In short, they are part of the church community in every way. "A few people had reservations at first," Associate Pastor Nancy McCurley recounts, "but no one does now. Some have admitted that they were wrong and now feel great about our new sense of community." Hillsboro wants to be an inspiration and a challenge to other churches that could do the same thing. "These people have special gifts that we don't have. Instead of just serving them, we are being enriched in ways we couldn't have guessed."

Hospitality, Shelter for Visitors
Greek Orthodox Church of St. George, Bethesda, Maryland

In the early 1970s, the National Institutes of Health, just outside Washington, D.C., started a program to treat congenital heart disease in children. Many of the children that came were from Greece, where there were no facilities for open heart surgery. While the stay and treatment at NIH was free, there were no provisions made for the children's families, who were often of moderate means, did not speak English, and were generally overwhelmed by trying to deal with a large American city.

The Greek Orthodox Church of St. George responded to their needs. A member of the church donated funds to create Kollecas House, a house built in St. George's courtyard where families can stay in a home-like environment. The visiting children and their families always get a friendly, helpful reception from St. George's congregation, receiving food, financial

above: Kollecas house as seen from the sanctuary. left: George Hatzikos and his mother in the kitchen of the house. They have just arrived from Greece for treatment. He has been coming to NIH since he was five. below: Julia Plomasen, primary contact person between visiting families and the church.

assistance, transportation, translation help and emotional support. Key to the success of the church's efforts is Julia Plomasen, who is often the family's primary contact.

Research programs at NIH have changed over the years and so has the Kollecas House program. The one constant, however, is the unfailing hospitality offered by this congregation. As Father George Papaioanou says, "Becoming involved has its rewards. You will receive a lot more than you will give."

Transitional Housing...in the Church
University Baptist Church, Seattle, Washington

With a long history of providing sanctuary in its building for refugees from El Salvador and Guatemala, this very active church has expanded its activities to meet needs of people in its own area. The two dormer windows poking through the roof are part of a renovation that turned unused third floor space into two transitional apartments for homeless women with children.

University Baptist's housing effort is part of the Homelessness Project of the Church Council of Greater Seattle. Congregations provide the shelter (generally in houses they own) and the Project provides staff services. Families are referred to the Project by local emergency family shelters and carefully screened before being accepted for stays of up to 18 months in the housing.

90 Days' Free Housing and a Chance to Break Out of Poverty

White Memorial Presbyterian Church, Raleigh, North Carolina

"We've been on a pretty steep learning curve for over three years now," is how director Ginger Webb describes the experience of trying to change people's lives through a creative transitional housing program.

Four years ago, church pastor Ed Pickard went to a conference in Dallas, where he heard of a church providing transitional housing as a way to break the cycle of poverty. He liked the approach, and his church got excited enough by the idea to send a team of people back to Texas to learn all they could about how it worked. With some creative changes to make the model work in Raleigh, the church worked quickly to establish Step-Up Ministries.

The program tries to be a one-time intervention in a family's life. It is not a band-aid, but a catalyst for change. A homeless family or a family trying to escape a bad public housing situation, or a broken family or a battered woman and her children, can sign up for the program, which will provide them with an apartment rent-free, including free utilities, for 90 days. The family must have some income from employment. When they enter the program, they must sign a commitment that obligates them to undertake several things. First, each family must put one-half of its income each week into a special savings fund. Families must attend regular counseling and teaching sessions on budgeting, home management, shopping skills and employment. While adults attend those sessions, children take part in a youth services program. Each family is assigned a sponsoring family from the church to provide some social contacts. At the end of the 90 days, families are given substantial help in finding apartments of their own, and they have their savings fund for rent or deposits.

It is hoped that, by the end of the program, families also have acquired some skills and understanding for managing their lives. The emphasis is on not allowing people to become dependent on the program or its staff, but on building egos and capabilities and independence. A program staff member follows up on families for a year after they are out on their own, and the track record so far is impressive. In a little over three years, the program has helped 35 families break out of poverty.

As Ms. Webb says, "We all get such a sense of accomplishment from giving people a chance to 'step up' and change their lives for the better."

People from the congregation, Step-Up families and volunteers join in a prayer circle at the church.

The duplex donated by a congregation member.

Setting Up Transitional Housing and Services in a Former Men's Rest Home

Pawtucket Congregational Church, UCC, Pawtucket, Rhode Island

Reverend George Peters reflects on the beginnings of his church's outreach efforts this way: "When I first went to Pawtucket, the church wanted to focus on the church growth issue. After some years of decline, we were very concerned about the need for membership growth. We began to work on that, but we were too focused on it, and it became clear to me that if we were to grow as a church we needed to develop a ministry to the community."

To help define the most effective way to serve their community, the church asked a student to survey community leaders, church members, and people on the street, about their views on the "most pressing unmet social need in Pawtucket." The answer: housing and homelessness.

Though the beds are set close together, this bedroom affords privacy to a family.

Rather than simply plunging in on their own, church leaders asked a worker with the Pawtucket Community Action Program to meet with them a few times. After learning a lot more about the problem, the church's Board of Christian Mission decided it might best serve as a convener of all of the interested parties. For six months, every other week, people from mental health and human service agencies, the mayor's office and the Salvation Army met with the Board.

In early 1985, the church, with all its partners, rented an apartment to shelter one homeless family at a time until they could get back on their feet and find housing. Some services were provided by the other partners, but the church raised the money. Eventually, with a small state grant, a foundation grant, and lots of fundraising efforts, the program increased to four apartments and employed its first full-time director, Marsha Correa.

from left: staffer Travis Roy, current executive director Elaine Coderre, and resident Michael C. Woodward.

The apartments were scattered to avoid problems with any one neighborhood or attaching a stigma to living in a shelter. In time, it was decided that consolidation was more important to coordinate social services. Using a state grant for a portion of the needed funds, the shelter purchased a building. A mortgage was hard to get until the church threatened to withdraw its endowment funds from their bank. The bank became more cooperative.

In the beginning, everything functioned through the church, but "it was always our goal to establish a new entity," says Reverend Peters. In time, the Emergency Shelter of Pawtucket and Central Falls was set up as a non-profit corporation with its own board of directors. It bought a former men's nursing home that accommodates up to 35 people in seven sleeping areas for as long as ten weeks. The program also helps people manage their money, find and keep a job, and re-enter the world with some confidence and stability. Because of these services and the overall approach, this "shelter" is really more like transitional housing.

Urging Banks to Re-Invest in the Community
Congregations in Brooklyn, through Brooklyn Ecumenical Cooperatives, Brooklyn, New York

Members of the Brooklyn Ecumenical Cooperatives meet with bank representatives to discuss community lending policies.

This book is mostly about projects and programs for individual congregations or small groups of them, acting together. But when there's a big problem, only a big group with major resources and a forceful approach may be able to solve it. In this case, it's 43 Brooklyn congregations, a hospital and some schools, all working through Brooklyn Ecumenical Cooperatives (BEC), to which they belong and pay dues.

The major objectives: to convince major New York banks to make more loans in low income areas, to increase the supply of affordable housing and enable people to buy it. Their resources: the 300 million dollars their institutions and individuals have on deposit in those banks. Their approach: community-based, persistent, politically savvy, and direct. Representing 40,000 member families, 80% of whom are Latino or African-American, BEC runs on about $200,000 a year, half in dues, the rest from grants and other resources

The setting for one of their most direct approaches was the basement of a large church in the Fort Greene area of Brooklyn, with 400 BEC delegates and the representatives of six banks in attendance.

As *New York Newsday* described the meeting, "teams of negotiators, including ministers, teachers, unemployed workers and retirees, quizzed the bankers about their community lending policies and urged them to lend more money in low-income neighborhoods." As one of BEC's staff said: "People are really impressed with how 'prepped' our people are. It's not just rhetoric. It's very concrete, we know what we want."

As for the meeting's success in getting people to understand each other, the same staffer said, "People are fighting for their neighborhood. And if you're sitting across from a banker, CitiBank has a face!"

The result was a commitment by the banks to do more, including: programs for low-to-moderate income first-time home buyers; low down payments; and a higher debt-to-income ratio for mortgage eligibility.

But the success came not just from one big meeting. There were many other meetings and negotiations, much media coverage and even support from Congressional representatives. And the agreement goes beyond Brooklyn: the banks will give greater attention to other lower income areas of the city as well.

BEC started in 1979 as a cooperative of a few churches to buy heating fuel at lower prices, in response to the energy crisis. But it has gone far beyond that and today can list as accomplishments a credit union, a capital bank to finance affordable housing and small businesses, and a significant amount of housing rehabilitation.

Next, it's jobs that BEC will tackle. Among other things, it will be looking to the banks for loans and grants to finance small business start-ups. "You can't even think about making a down payment without work, so that's our next step."

Congregations and Individuals Investing their Dollars in the Community

Congregations in Winchester, Massachusetts, through the Boston Community Loan Fund

It's a beautiful spring morning, and people are boarding a small chartered bus outside the Epiphany Episcopal church in Boston's affluent suburb of Winchester. They're Christians and Jews, members of a town team of a half dozen Winchester congregations bound for Boston on a common mission: to see what kind of housing results their money can buy.

Responding to Winchester's interest in "doing something about housing," the tour is being sponsored by the Boston Community Loan Fund. Under the guidance of BCLF staff member Jeanne DuBois, these eighteen people are visiting city neighborhoods where many have never been, to see how investments from throughout the Boston area have made over 1,000 units of excellent affordable housing a reality.

BCLF has a superb track record in helping create and upgrade affordable housing while building community. It's one of many private, non-profit community loan funds throughout the country (see *Resources* section) that make below-market-rate loans to help finance affordable housing and/or business start-ups.

above left: Jeanne Dubois of BCLF describes the tour as the group prepares to leave Winchester. above: First stop in Boston's South End is at a group home for recovering substance abusers.

The basic principle is simple. An individual, congregation or organization makes a gift or loan to BCLF. If a loan, it's at a low interest rate. BCLF then lends this money to community-based organizations which will build or rehabilitate housing units and make them available to lower income people.

The key to success is the fund's ability to be a good manager, ensuring low investment risk. In eight years, the BCLF has had no loan losses, and investors have shown their confidence by reinvesting at a 72% overall rollover rate.

By the bus trip's end, the Winchester people will have visited four types of housing. They'll have met some of the people who created it and who live there, as well as enthusiastic investors who will affirm their sense that this is vital — and do-able. They will also have proof that even modest investments, when combined, can accomplish things far beyond the means of a single individual or congregation.

Checking back on the Winchester congregations awhile after the bus tour, substantial financial commitments both by congregations and by individuals are in the works or have actually been made!

Taking to the Streets Against Drugs

First African Methodist Episcopal Church, Los Angeles, California

The big church in the heart of Los Angeles has met the problem of drugs head-on. "We won't eliminate the drug problem entirely," says pastor Dr. Cecil Murray, "but we have to eliminate the spinoffs: children killing children, adults killing children, neighborhoods held in bondage and terror, school dropout rates of 50 percent, drive-by shootings...." For the last seven years, this church has engaged in an ambitious community reclamation program.

Along with its many other programs, the church's Richard Allen Men's Society has taken to the streets. Working successively through four different sections of the city, 40 to 150 men walk the streets each Friday, Saturday and Sunday, from 8:00 p.m. until midnight. They target known "rock houses," fortified homes where crack cocaine is sold. They video tape drug deals and surround houses to cut off business. The men also go door-to-door to other homes, offering the church's services to residents of the embattled neighborhoods. The marchers have been joined at times by the mayor of L.A. (a church member), deputy police chiefs and a city councilor. Each patrol has been accompanied by police officers who are also church members who have requested this special assignment. Twenty-five other predominantly black churches have been recruited to support the campaign.

Mark Whitlock, president of First AME's Richard Allen Men's Society, in front of a former crack house that the church shut down, and turned back into a regular neighborhood home.

The effort has not been without its dangers. The marchers have been threatened by drug dealers, occasionally pelted with rocks and were once pinned to the ground by gun fire for 20 minutes. On this occasion the accompanying police officers urged the church walkers to turn back. The men huddled quickly and decided to march on. Within a few minutes, residents in neighboring buildings came out and joined them. Forty men quickly multiplied into 200 people. That kind of swelling support from residents has overcome the threat to safety, and, to date, no one has been hurt.

In the patrolled areas, police report a 65% drop in the crime rate. So far eight crack houses have been permanently closed down. Three of the houses have been bought and rehabilitated by the church. Deputy Police Chief William Rathburn, who accompanied one of the marches, comments: "They create a very formidable force. This is what we need, people to stand up and say, 'I'm not going to allow these things to take place in my neighborhood.'" While a patrol group stood with placards in front of a rock house (accompanied by the mayor), the owner of the property drove up and was so impressed by the scene that he agreed to clean out the drug dealers and renovate the house for affordable housing.

Battling Drugs Door to Door
Mt. Nebo A.M.E. Church, College Station, Arkansas

"Our motto is one by one, house by house, we're going to beat this problem, "says Linda Henson, leader of an anti-drug campaign at the Mt. Nebo AME Church. Every afternoon during the summer months, Ms. Henson and her group of children and adults can be seen marching through the streets of their Little Rock neighborhood carrying placards in their fight against drugs. At the house of someone they know has a drug problem, they stop, ask permission to say a prayer, and invite that person to join their march and their group. With many, the invitation works. The group marches up every street and passes every house.

The effort is called the College Station Drug Awareness Program. Every Wednesday night, approximately 60 people, mostly kids and young adults, meet to talk about the issues they are struggling with —the biggest topic is always drugs. People come from seven area churches, as well as from the group's marches. There are usually adult guest speakers, many of whom have had drug or alcohol problems, who talk to the young people about how to make good life decisions.

"Kids need opportunities to go places together and have fun with each other if they are going to be able to trust and rely on each other."

Linda Henson, volunteer

Pulling the Religious Community Together to Combat Drug and Alcohol Abuse
Second Baptist Church, Little Rock, Arkansas

The city of Little Rock, with help from a planning grant from the Robert Wood Johnson Foundation, has started Fight Back, a large-scale program to fight drug and alcohol abuse.

Second Baptist played a significant role in the effort. Church members sent out over 200 letters to congregations and religious organizations, asking them to get involved and to take up special offerings. They raised over $100,000. Many offered use of their facilities, got involved in educational efforts, and served as referral sources. Fight Back has grown from this full-scale involvement. "Our people got mobilized," says pastor Billy White. "This campaign is something that can draw all of the religious communities together into one effort with the city."

Neighborhood support centers are being created to provide ongoing services to people of any age. A neighborhood alert system will be related to each center to coordinate police coverage and city services within each neighborhood. This single comprehensive assault on the city's substance abuse problems seems to be working. In the most difficult areas of the city where the alert center program is already functioning, it is reported that crime has declined by 33 percent.

Rebuilding Their Neighborhood, Reclaiming Their Community
Bethel AME Church, Birmingham, Alabama

"You can't invite everyone to celebrate the victory at the end if it hasn't been everybody's battle all along."

Reverend Ron Norad (above)

"Neighborhood folks are reclaiming their community and their way of life," says Reverend Ron Norad, describing what is happening around his church in the Ensley neighborhood of Birmingham.

Just a few years ago, Bethel AME sat in the middle of an economically depressed, six-block neighborhood dominated by dilapidated houses and overgrown vacant lots. Then the church got interested in Reverend Norad's idea for change. The key to success, he felt, was an emphasis on community and a common sense of ownership from the beginning.

The pastor and congregation members went door-to-door and spoke with every family in the neighborhood. They discussed problems, needs and ideas. All residents were invited to community meetings at the church. Everybody felt included in the process, even before it was clear what direction it might take.

The result of the process was the BEAT project—the Bethel Ensley Action Taskforce. A non-profit housing corporation modeled after some aspects of the Habitat for Humanity program, BEAT set out to restore and rebuild the entire six-block area using primarily volunteer labor. The church wanted not "just to build housing, but to recreate a community." All along the way, community people took lead roles. Area churches were first asked to make financial commitments as well as substantial commitments of volunteer labor. The next step was networking with agencies and locating financial resources. A large grant came from Greater Birmingham ministries, allowing purchase of much of the property. Eventually, the city cooperated with a $3 million bond issue to finance public improvements in the area.

The work has gone rapidly forward. A team of 14 architects meets weekly to create plans and oversee the work. Money and labor from other churches continue to arrive. Over 20 churches or corporations have made the "full" commitment of $30,000 each. One church provided over 200 volunteers, including both skilled and unskilled labor.

Virtually every resident of the neighborhood has pitched in. The city is repairing streets and installing or upgrading streetlights, sewers and sidewalks. Working side-by-side with people from all over the Birmingham area, residents are building homes they will have an opportunity to own. Financing has been pre-arranged, allowing families to purchase the new houses. Excitement is high in and around the church. "Both church and community are being reborn," says Reverend Norad.

A Community Center is the Heart of the Neighborhood

St. Paul's Baptist Church, Philadelphia, Pennsylvania

For three decades the Cunningham Community Center has been just that: the center of its community's life. "We try to deal with the total needs and life of our neighborhood," says Center Director Gloria Whiting. The Center belongs to and is a sorely needed outreach of inner city St. Paul's Baptist Church. Built in 1952, it was the dream of the late Reverend E. Luther Cunningham, former pastor of the church.

The center's programs offer a wide range of services. There are children's drama and dance groups. Older kids can learn sewing and cooking skills. A large gym in the Center is filled with teams competing in any of several youth recreational basketball leagues. In the summer the Center becomes a large academic enrichment program offering cultural field trips and diverse experiences.

There is a full-time day care program for 40 preschoolers. Fifty elementary aged children are enrolled in after-school programs where they get help with homework, reading enrichment and language arts. The Center sponsors family workshops, casework counseling and a referral service. Job training takes place all year round, but very heavily in the summer. People in the community who might otherwise have ended up on welfare, are employed in a variety of jobs and are taught job skills they can take with them to other employers.

Literally hundreds of lives are touched by these programs every year. It has become the neighborhood's focus in many ways.

This kind of program is expensive to run. Blessed with a large multi-purpose building already paid for, the church uses the facility to raise some of the money it needs. The building is rented out periodically for wedding receptions, various community functions, and is the site for a number of fundraisers throughout the year. Other sources of funding include the United Way and small foundation grants, but over half of the $125,000 budget still comes right out of the budget of St. Paul's Church.

Cunningham Community House is the result of a long term commitment that has been sustained by a congregation that wants to be at the heart of its community, even though most of its members no longer live in the immediate neighborhood. "There's really a sense of loyalty," says St. Paul's pastor, Reverend Arthur L. Johnson. "Actually, the church is a mission in the community. We have a commitment here, this is where our roots are."

Executive Director Gloria Whiting is shown here in front of a painting of the Cunningham Center with Recreational Director Jerome "Butch" Mills, who grew up in the neighborhood.

Embracing Their Community:
It All Started with a Grapefruit Truck
Santa Fe Episcopal, San Antonio, Texas

Not so many years ago, weekly services with a handful of worshippers were the only signs of life at Santa Fe Episcopal Church. An Anglican church in a Mexican-American neighborhood, it was on the verge of closing its doors.

Things started to change under the leadership of a Hispanic priest, Carmen Guerrera. Noticing that a large number of people waited in front of the church each week for a grapefruit truck that distributed free fruit, the priest invited them in to wait where it was warm. And she talked with them about their faith, about their needs, and about what they wanted in a church. Before long, many began to meet for Bible study an hour before the grapefruit truck arrived. They were joined by others and continued meeting well after the grapefruit harvest.

As real life issues were raised, people were encouraged to act on them and to consider the church as a way to make their faith concrete. Soon the church became a place where people came to donate and cook food for neighbors, to start a head start program tailored to the needs of migrant workers' children, to set up high school equivalence training, to have a latchkey program where kids are cared for by neighborhood grandmothers until parents finish their work day.

above: Santa Fe summer program for seniors also takes a meal to 30 shut-in seniors. below: Susie Bruni, a member of Santa Fe, previously handled immigration matters for members of the community, and currently helps people get utility assistance.

The church continues to grow in community spirit and outreach and, as current rector Reverend Will Waters says, "It's truly the lay people who are the ongoing story of this church, a story of empowerment and transformation of lay people into folks who can give workshops, take on officials, deal with domestic violence. They're no different from other people, but they've had leadership training and been given the opportunity to have a voice."

Today Santa Fe is a partner in Project Rebuild, through which volunteers repair, paint, and clean homes and yards in the neighborhood. There are Alcoholics Anonymous and Al Anon groups, and classes in literacy, citizen preparation, and English as a second language. The old vicarage is the site for a support group for battered women and for a program for kids at risk because one of their parents has been in prison. And along with all this outreach to its community has come a revitalization of the worship life of the church, with more than a hundred participating with spirited Hispanic music on Sunday mornings.

Young Adults Get Involved in Their Neighborhood
St. Anne Roman Catholic Church, Santa Ana, California

Saint Anne is a large, predominantly Hispanic parish in a lower-income section of the city. Its neighborhood is troubled by gangs and drugs. A young adult group of over 200 at the church, the Jovenes para Cristo (Youth for Christ), is trying to make a difference.

The Jovenes run rehabilitation retreats for people involved with drugs, for young people in gangs, and for others in the area who want help. Up to a month before each retreat, Jovenes members take to the streets every day to convince gang members and others to come.

The Jovenes have developed a whole process that deepens the group spiritually. "The work of this group just keeps growing and emerging," says Father Joseph Justice. "I just let people do their thing. They have a momentum of their own."

St. Anne's has also helped found an interdenominational community organizing network to try to change city policies and marshal more resources to make long-term changes in the lives of the poor. The church organized and hosted the first of a series of meetings with district police commanders; over 500 community residents attended. "All of the initiative here is from the lay people," says Father Justice. "They take responsibility for the programs and when things don't work, they make changes. Their faith and commitment make everything happen."

Father Joseph Justice (second from left) with some of his parishioners.

Re-Connecting with Their Neighborhood
Trinity United Methodist Church, Des Moines, Iowa

Parish nurse Darleen Sickert (right) visits the home of Martha and Rozlyn Rankin.

Located in an inner city neighborhood with a lot of serious problems, Trinity's membership was diminishing and the church was becoming merely a convenient site for outreach programs. Though extremely valuable, the programs had become separate from the congregation's life and were being run by people from outside the church. Commented the former pastor, Reverend Brian Carter, "The programs became programs to and for the community. . . instead of programs with the community. Trinity lost contact with its neighborhood."

When the organization sponsoring the programs was dissolved, Trinity saw an opportunity to redeem the situation. In 1990, the church made a "recommitment, to continue and expand our justice ministries in ways to meet the needs of Trinity's neighbors and that enable Trinity to reconnect with its neighborhood." Church members met monthly with residents to discuss how to improve housing, increase home ownership, respond to crime and drugs and build self-esteem and community pride.

In just a year, average worship attendance had nearly doubled, membership was up 30 percent. In a church of under 100, the numbers aren't yet impressive, but the enthusiasm is. As the pastor wrote, "Trinity is a new congregation." Building membership and expanding mission outreach are going hand in hand.

Other Possibilities:

KAM Isaiah Israel, Chicago, Illinois, as part of an inter-neighborhood coalition, Partners in Community Development, has **adopted a public housing project** and held paint-a-thons in which its volunteers spruce up the project.

First Presbyterian Church, Broadalbin, New York, triumphed over local zoning and environmental challenges and some neighborhood resistance in its rural community and **built needed housing for the elderly** with state and federal funds. Key in cinching the project's success was the willingness of a member of the congregation to sell the church an eight-acre parcel of land at well below its worth.

Tenth Memorial Baptist Church, Philadelphia, Pennsylvania, is one of many urban congregations which have **built multi-story, affordable housing complexes** in their neighborhoods using public funds. These developments provide both housing and sorely needed jobs in maintenance and other services. Tenth Memorial, which even provided land for the housing, also **bought and renovated a row house across the street** from it, with its own funds.

New ideas of your own?
Projects you like?
Jot them down on p. 97.

Beyond
Your Community

Imagine a congregation making tractors and shipping them to farmers in Central America! That's quite a reach beyond one's own community. While that congregation's mission is probably unique, in concept it's no different from making quilts and sending them to people who need warm bedding.

The communities that you might reach out to could be in another country, or another part of the United States, downstate, or simply across town in an area you know little about.

Pairing with a "sister congregation" encourages a commitment to a long-term relationship, both with the congregation and its community.

Hosting a "pilgrimage" to enable people from comfortable lifestyles to experience what it means to be in need, and to do something about it, is an excellent, effective way to get people to open their hearts and minds and reach out.

Reverend Beal takes some kids in Johnstown, Pennsylvania, on a ride on a MUV (Mission Utility Vehicle) before it is shipped off to Central America (see story p. 84)

Exporting your capabilities — whether it's a youth group going to a work camp in Appalachia or a medical team traveling to Honduras — can touch needs that may be deeper than those nearby. Providing sanctuary for victims of oppressive regimes is still another way to reach out to people beyond your community, people who are in dire need of you.

"Twinning" with a Personal Touch
Holy Spirit Parish, Fargo, North Dakota

They call it a "twinning" arrangement. Holy Spirit Parish in North Dakota (above right), a medium-sized, mostly white, middle-income church, has intertwined its life with a small, low-income, black parish in Mississippi (above left). A unique long-distance relationship has developed that has enriched both congregations.

For a number of years, Holy Spirit provided some financial support for the ministry of a nun associated with its parish. A few years ago she moved her ministry to several black parishes in Mississippi, where she helps poor mothers and run-away teenage girls, delivering babies and promoting a healthy environment for the newborns. The direction of Holy Spirit's mission shifted with her, and the two congregations twinned.

School supplies, baby clothes and quilts, clothing and other goods are sent south. Families in North Dakota also "adopt" particular families in Mississippi. The adoptions are not anonymous. Many Holy Spirit parishioners are involved with the same family through the years. When possible, they get each family member's size and learn individual needs. Letters and photos are exchanged. In fact, these personal connections

have led individuals in the parish to donate money to put two young Mississippi women through nurses' training.

"People get excited and energized by this connection," says Father Phillip Ackerman, Holy Spirit's priest. "They are willing to support this because they feel like they have come to know the people personally."

Every other year, to keep things "personal," several people from Holy Spirit go to Mississippi to visit and exchange news, and on alternate years Holy Spirit finances a trip to North Dakota for someone from their partner church.

Embracing as a friend from Mississippi leaves Fargo North, Dakota. The congregations alternate years visiting each other.

Making MUVs & Giving them to the Third World
Summit Chapel United Methodist Church, Johnstown, Pennsylvania

In the MUV workshop in Johnstown, Pennsylvania.

A MUV in use in Guatemala.

It's hard to imagine what mechanics and a machine shop have to do with church outreach. At Summit Chapel the connection is strong and clear. It's called a MUV—Mission Utility Vehicle, a unique, three-wheeled, all-terrain utility vehicle made by Summit Chapel for use by church and relief workers in the Third World.

In 1988, Reverend Raymond Beal and his church borrowed an idea and some technology from a program in Missouri. Noting the dramatic need for transportation in the Third World, a retired United Methodist mission project worker designed a special vehicle to suit the needs he had seen first-hand. A group of volunteers from Summit Chapel went to Missouri to see the operation and to draw plans of the MUV for production in Pennsylvania.

The Johnstown area has been hit hard by the decline of the local steel industry. Reverend Beal was convinced that in a community rich with metal-working skills and people needing work, building MUVs could serve a dual role.

A small church a few blocks away closed its doors for lack of members and donated its building to Summit Chapel to serve as the machine shop. It was called Cast-Off Ministries. One full-time worker was hired to run the shop and oversee teams of volunteers.

Area churches were solicited for $3,500 to $4,500 each to sponsor the building and shipment of each MUV. Reverend Beal reports that churches which had not had a great deal of enthusiasm for outreach efforts in the past became very enthusiastic about "something that they could see and touch being created with their gifts. It inspires churches to think that there is something concrete that they can actually do." Reverend Beal and other volunteers take a sample vehicle around to sponsoring churches on Sunday mornings so people can get a first-hand look at what they are underwriting. Other churches have lent support by sending crews to help with some of the work.

In a part of the country where the population is in steep decline and many churches are closing, Summit Chapel is rapidly adding members. Reverend Beal attributes much of that directly to the MUV program. "People are attracted to a church that is committed enough to continue to reach out, even in tough times. Even when they are hurting themselves, our people still want to give to others."

Declaring Sanctuary

KAM Isaiah Israel Congregation
Chicago, Illinois

KAM has worked hard, not only to provide help for people in need but also to do so in a way that "promotes social change," says past Social Action chair Sidney Hollander, "not just among those we help, but in our congregation as well." The synagogue has tried to cross and overcome social and racial boundaries in its work. One of the ways it started in that direction was as a "sanctuary" congregation.

In late 1986, the Social Action Committee started to debate providing sanctuary for Central American refugees as a way, to help people who were fleeing for their lives and to spur the congregation to engage directly in the issue of U.S. involvement in that region. After a year of discussion which included hearing from experts with diverse points of view, the temple's board voted almost unanimously for a "Declaration of Sanctuary." Within two months, a request came to provide that sanctuary.

For almost two years, the congregation hosted a woman and her two daughters who were refugees from Guatemala. Almost all of the other members of the woman's family had been killed, and consid-erable aid and emotional support were needed to help her to recover and to adjust. A member of the congregation donated an apartment, rent free. One hundred other donors provided $18 per month to support the family. The refugee family's presence did indeed keep the political issue alive in the temple community in a constructive way.

The family's story had a happy ending. After two years, the woman married an American man. The chair of the Social Action Committee returned with her to Guatemala (a scary journey) and obtained a visa for her to return legally to the U.S.. She is now a valued member of the community, working as a caregiver for infants infected with the HIV virus.

KAM Social Action Committee members and the Guatemalan family.

An Ongoing Health Care Mission
with One Village in Honduras
Community Church, Franconia, New Hampshire

6:30 a.m. Sunday. Logan Airport, Boston. American Airlines flight 1291 is about to depart for Honduras. Duffel bags of clothing and medical supplies abound, including some being transported for Jesuit friends.

"This is my first time going there. I'm really excited!" One member of the six-person group hasn't shown up yet. Oh, there she is! A hug, smiles, a last bite of a donut, and off they race, bound for Honduras.

Many churches send people to work in other countries, but the Franconia Community Church has gone further. "We wanted to be a mission partnership with one village where we could make a difference in an ongoing way," says pastor Paula Wolcott.

For eight years this church has sent mission teams recruited from the church and the community to the village of El Rosario, Honduras, for two weeks, every other month. The program is called ACTS, Americans Caring, Teaching, Sharing. The work teams pay their own airfare and expenses. Church funds and donations go directly to supplies or equipment, or to meet other needs in El Rosario.

Each team has at least one doctor or dentist. The church, working with local volunteers, has set up a medical clinic, stocked with medicines donated by drug companies or bought with church funds.

(above) Dr. Wolcott, third from right, and his team at Logan Airport. (right) In El Rosario working on a latrine.

Hondurans are trained to promote preventive health and dental care. Ten women are being taught to be health promoters in their own villages. Equipped with basic supplies and medicine, they are trained to provide rudimentary services.

Mission teams have also completed two gravity fed clean-water systems, and they have two systems planned for outlying villages. The goal of providing a latrine for each family in the village is almost accomplished. The teams are also looking forward to a number of agricultural projects.

In the spirit of partnership, everything the teams do is turned over for village people to run. To make that goal possible, teams have provided training in bookkeeping, decision making, and basic management.

Since 1985, over 30 teams have given time to this Honduran village. "Everyone has had an amazing learning experience," says the pastor. "The local people were skeptical at first, but now it has become a real two-way partnership." All of this activity from a church of just over a hundred members.

A Deep Understanding of Service
Orland Presbyterian Church, Orland, Pennsylvania

Like thousands of youth groups, these high schoolers and their leaders from this suburban church have come away from a week in Appalachia working in five-person crews on house repairs, having had more than just fun. Better than a narrative, these quotes from a conversation with the six young people shown at right provide insights into their experience.

"We've been doing it eight years in this church . . . different places . . . part of what you realize is when you get there, no matter where you are, people need help, and there's need all around.

"It's a lot of fun being able to help someone else, and you get really close to your resident."

"It's neat when you get done, because you have accomplished something and you feel good inside that you did something to help somebody else. Every time I go I feel very appreciative of what I have at home. This one lady a couple of years ago had a refrigerator outside and she had barely any food in it, and she washed all her dishes in a creek next to her house. I was, like, well, I have a dishwasher and my refrigerator's inside my house, and I have two of them, and it just makes me feel like . . . it's not right."

"A lot of time the reaction of residents is: 'You're doing this for free!?' The kids get a kick out of telling them, 'No,' and they're astonished when you explain you pay to do this" [group members pay their own transportation].

"We are there not only to meet needs, but just to be with these people! A lot are lonely...that's a real big part of it, just loving these people."

". . . you think you do it to have fun, to get away, to see a different part of the country, hang with friends, but after the end of a week what you went for is not what you got out of it. How you would answer that question on Monday and on Saturday would be totally different. I'd probably say on Saturday I went as a servant of God to do a little part of His work."

"You leave with a lot of great experiences. . . the best part was being with the people. . . then at night they have fantastic programs that bring you to a deeper understanding of what service is all about . . ."

"My friends think I'm kind of crazy, like, why would you work and not get paid and why would you pay? ....What's the point of all that? Then you show people before and after shots and they're, like, whoa!"

top: An Orland group at work in Appalachia. middle: Recent work camp participants. above: A work camp worker and a resident make friends.

Understanding Poverty and Need: "The Pilgrimage" Crosses Boundaries, Finds Common Ground

Church of the Pilgrims, Washington, D.C.

"We always have to keep in mind where we are and what that means." This is the way Patricia Goldner sums up her view of the outreach philosophy of the Church

James Duddy (in glasses) a "pilgrim" from Saco, Maine, talks with Chester R. Hollinsworth, a homeless man who is having lunch at S.O.M.E. soup kitchen.

of the Pilgrims. "Where they are" is in the heart of Washington, D. C. "What that means" is that there are opportunities and extraordinary needs all around them.

The most unusual of the church's many outreach programs is "The Pilgrimage," established in 1972 to make the most of its location. At that time, the church was a congregation in decline, located in a changing urban neighborhood. It had a huge historic building and a vital location, but there were very few parishioners.

The church envisioned a new role for itself: providing access to the realities and resources of the city to all those who live far from a city or have chosen the more sheltered world of the suburbs. As they conceived it, The Pilgrimage would be both a study center and a "hands-on" experience with the city and its people in need.

Over the last two decades, groups have come from far and wide for a weekend or longer, to visit and work at shelters and soup kitchens, to learn about urban issues, to explore faith issues. During their stay, they participate in church-designed programs or they design programs of their own.

The church provides dormitory rooms, a kitchen, dining facilities and meeting space. It is church volunteers who have put in the labor to renovate part of the education wing to house the center. Church people also serve as hosts, guides, resources, and teachers. Donations and fees from pilgrimage groups pay for a staff coordinator.

A typical group of "pilgrims" have come for a week, from Saco, Maine, to witness urban needs first hand and take a turn at serving. They're high school students — curious, energetic, and thoughtful. They listen with intense sympathy

"You hear about the ghetto and people getting shot and it makes it so you don't want to go into those neighborhoods and you're afraid of those people. But ... you don't have to be afraid, they're just people, they're having a tough time, but they're people, like me."

Bill Brady, 18 year old pilgrim from Saco, Maine

as Beulah, a woman who has spent most of her life on the streets and who now helps street people, tells them her story. Afterwards they smother her with hugs, thanking her for sharing her life with them so openly, so effectively.

At the soup kitchen called S.O.M.E. (So Others Might Eat), the Saco pilgrims are a bit overwhelmed at first. But by lunch time they're right in sync. From the kitchen comes the yell, "Hot plate!", and the kids who are serving on line pick it right up: "Hot plate! Watch out, hot plate!" As the steaming pile of chicken is set down, they serve it onto plates and then give the plates to people who have come there to eat. Between shifts, they bustle about clearing and resetting the tables. On the way back to the church in the van they are talking up a storm: "Boy, that was really hard work, but it was really fun, too!" "Yeah, those people were so nice."

above : The Saco group on their way to visit Lazarus House, which is in the 14th street neighborhood of D.C.
right: Reverend Nathan Jernegen gives the Saco pilgrims a tour of Sojourner House, a community and educational center that has a food bank. below: Back at the church, the group gathers to discuss the day's work.

Other Possibilities:

Temple Beth Am, Merrick, New York, at Thanksgiving spearheads the effort to **run an interfaith newspaper ad**, supported and signed by congregations all over the metropolitan area and appealing to everyone to support the outreach work of their own congregation. Rabbi Ronald Brown, who conceived the idea, makes the annual appeal to the other congregations and religious organizations and places the ad.

Old Cambridge Baptist Church, Cambridge, Massachusetts, **gave sanctuary to a labor organizer** in Central America who was tortured, raped, and imprisoned several times and finally managed to escape her country. In addition to taking her into their community, **the church publicized the situation**, with her consent, to clarify the plight of others in her country. They also **rent office space in their building at reduced rates** to nonprofit organizations whose missions reflect and further the church's outreach objectives.

Central Congregational Church in Providence, Rhode Island, and Central Baptist in Wayne, Pennsylvania, are two of many congregations that have **shops which sell crafts produced by low income people living in such places as Appalachia, Africa, Central and South America**. Central Baptist's Crafts of Freedom Shop (see banner at right) is especially successful, thanks in part to the church's highly visible main street location.

New ideas of your own?
Projects you like?
Jot them down on p. 97.

Healing the World

Healing-the-World — or "Tikun Olam"* in Hebrew — is the big concept. It's not outreach on a limited basis — say, building a house, or doing an after-school program, or even rejuvenating a whole neighborhood. The idea is to do whatever you can to make things "right", to heal it all. It's the attitude of many of the more active congregations in this book.

Healing-the-world is not just the place to end up, it's the place to start. Adopting it as your philosophy will give your outreach efforts wings! Even if you're a newcomer to outreach and starting off with your first project, if you commit to being "world fixers" you will soon find the spirit of outreach really taking hold.

And commitment is the key: to have a healing-the-world outlook means people must really "sign on". The stories here illustrate three important ways that congregation members can make that commitment.

(* pronounced tee-kun o-lahm)

Embracing the Metropolitan Area

Central Baptist Church, Wayne, Pennsylvania

"Outreach has become the central focus of this church," says Central Baptist pastor Dr. Stephen Jones. "We work to keep it balanced with a strong worship and spiritual life, but much of the energy and commitment we have comes from outreach." A church of only 260 members in the affluent "Main Line" suburbs of Philadelphia, Central Baptist has 13 "mission groups," clusters of people with a passion about a particular issue or need confronting their faith (some mission group members, with their banners, are pictured at the beginning of this section).

On a Sunday morning in February 1992, the congregation went a step further, meeting to adopt a "regional plan" of 10 initiatives focusing on needs it sees in its larger community, metropolitan Philadelphia. Its action stemmed from a forum sponsored by the Metropolitan Christian Council the previous month to examine the responsibilities of suburban congregations.

Among the 10 initiatives are: endorsing a "Declaration of Regional Interdependence," declaring the church as a racism-free zone; joining seven other congregations in the Main Line Interfaith Hospitality Network to house homeless families; continuing support and involvement in Habitat projects (see p. 65); taking an annual communion offering for a human services program of the city of Philadelphia; challenging its members to deposit a total of $50,000 in the minority-owned United Bank (see p. 59); supporting moderate and low income housing; and supporting other congregations making regional commitments.

To the city's gratitude but also surprise, Central Baptist immediately followed through on an initiative by sending $2,500, their communion offering, to support the city's rental voucher program for formerly homeless women and children (one Sunday a month the church's collection goes to a different outreach project; the congregation gives generously).

Other progress to date includes surpassing its $50,000 United Bank deposit goal, and co-founding the Delaware Valley Ecumenical Council, which Dr. Jones describes as "a highly effective activist group already getting results in the arena of racism in our metropolitan area and state government."

"We live in one of the area's richest suburbs, but we provide almost no services to the homeless who originate in our midst. We give to the city to assist with the inordinate social burdens city taxpayers face." Reverend Jones, in the letter accompanying the $2,500 check sent to the city by Central Baptist

Dr. Jones feels that both action and a public declaration such as Central Baptist made,

Thursday, March 12, 1992   THE SUBURBAN AND WAYNE TIMES   3-C

Central Baptist makes regional commitment

are necessary for suburban churches to be taken seriously in their commitment to living in solidarity with others in their wider community.

"If there is anything that CBC is doing that is unique, it is as a suburban church. If we redefine anything, we're redefining how to be a suburban church and be engaged with the broken edges of God's world."

Joining the Church and Committing to "Go Beyond the Walls"

First AME Church, Los Angeles, California

First AME, "FAME," whose story about combatting drugs is on p. 74, has received a lot of press coverage nationally because of its central role in the community during and after the 1992 troubles in South-Central Los Angeles. But this rapidly growing church of over 9,000 members has a long history of community involvement and a basic philosophy that everyone should make a commitment to go beyond the walls.

There are now 33 Beyond the Walls task forces, from adoptions and foster care to prison ministry, from skid row and homeless ministry to youth jobs and camping. The goals are high: Project Renaissance, whose executive director is First AME member Mark Whitlock (see p. 74), is committed to rebuilding Los Angeles.

As the church's pastor, Dr. Cecil Murray (shown on p. 127), says: "Membership training includes your commitment to a task force. You join a task force that takes the church beyond the walls. You aren't joining the church to save your soul. You join to save your soul and the soul of the community. We are here for personal salvation and for social salvation and all the rest is smoke . . . We try to offer so many things that if people leave here they can't say there was a deficit, they have to leave here because they say I really want to be a bench member and I'm not going to be accepted just sitting on the bench.

"Most churches are not really socially conscious . . . it seems such a waste, because every church—and your typical church in America has 250 members—that church has a teacher; someone in a medical field; someone in substance abuse; someone in the unions; somebody in journalism; somebody who can design a curriculum. Then just design your program to help children and the city. They'll feel good; everybody feels good when you're doing something worthwhile."

A group of new members

An Annual "Healing the World" Pledge

Kehillath Israel Jewish Congregation, Pacific Palisades, California

As every congregation knows, an individual commitment is the bottom line in doing outreach. From a congregation of just 425 families, Kehillath Israel has found a way to field hundreds of volunteers in its extensive social action activities: volunteers who work in shelters and homeless programs, teach people to read, tutor in a women's correctional facility, reach out to Russian immigrants, help people suffering from AIDS, and more.

Kehillath does this through an annual pledging program. What is pledged is not money, but time and effort. Although many congregations ask for such pledges, Kehillath's method is unique — and exceptionally successful.

The keys to this success are the kinds of commitments sought, and how the pledge card is designed and distributed. Every fall, on entering the synagogue for the high holy day services, each member or guest receives a "Tikun Olam" (Hebrew for "healing the world) pledge card. The card presents a dozen options for specific ways to volunteer, both in outreach programs and in other aspects of the congregation's life. The pledges on the card vary from year to year; a recent card is reproduced on the next page.

The card is designed with tear-off tabs, each with a specific pledge. People in the congregation tear off the tabs for the pledges they are willing to make and keep the tabs as a reminder of their commitments. Either at the end of the service or by mail, they return the rest of the card with its missing "teeth" to the synagogue. The tear-off feature not only makes the pledges more tangible, it also means that people who prefer not to write on the Jewish high holy days don't have to.

Kehillath's rabbi, Stephen Carr Reuben, devised the Tikun Olam card as a way for people to choose specific ways to serve. "We tried for years to make things happen with a generic social action committee, but the task is too big and amorphous. Now we get concrete, specific commitments for people to do practical work. Everyone feels like their time is well used, and they find many rewards for their efforts."

For many, as the quote on the card from the Talmud reads, "the reward for the Mitzvah is the Mitzvah itself," which translates as "the reward for the good deed is the good deed itself."

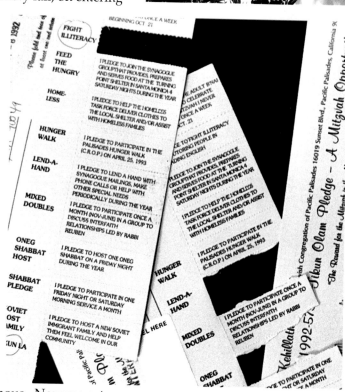

Tikun Olam cards returned to Kehillath with pledge tabs removed.

Kehillath Israel Jewish Congregation of Pacific Palisades • 16019 Sunset Boulevard, Pacific Palisades, California 90272

Tikun Olam Pledge—A Mitzvah Opportunity

"The Reward for the Mitzvah is the Mitzvah Itself" *Talmud*

Name _____

Address _____

Phone # (____) _____

Please fold and tear off at least one and return

SHABBAT PLEDGE	I pledge to attend one Friday or Saturday a month
SHARE YOUR PROFESSION	I pledge to meet with a Soviet Immigrant in my profession to help determine his/her job marketability and/or donate my services to help a new immigrant.
UNDERSTANDING RECONSTRUCTIONISM	I pledge to attend four Wednesday night sessions in January with Rabbi Reuben
SOVIET "WELCOME WAGON"	I pledge to become a "family friend" to a new Soviet Family, and invite them to join us for four synagogue services and/or events in the next 6 months
HEBREW LITERACY	I pledge to attend the one-day Hebrew Marathon (Oct. 14) or a class to learn to read Hebrew this year (Oct. 16 - Dec. 4)
HOMELESS	I pledge to attend a meeting of the K.I. Homeless Task Force, and/or volunteer at a homeless shelter
FEED THE HUNGRY	I pledge to help make and/or serve food to the homeless twice a month between 8-11 am or to pick up food donated to the Westside Drop-In Center, or deliver meals to the aged & home-bound.
AIDS PATIENTS SUPPORT	I pledge one Thursday morning a month to make sandwiches at K.I. then deliver them and talk with AIDS outpatients at County Hospital while they wait in line to see a doctor (so they won't lose their place in line)
FIGHT ILLITERACY	I pledge to tutor homeless children or illiterate adults in reading through Project Literacy
LEND-A-HAND	I pledge to lend a hand in the office and/or at a Temple event during the year
FAMILY TO FAMILY	I pledge to help make a new member feel welcome at KI by inviting them to a service or program once a month over the next six months.
TALMUD TORAH	I pledge to participate with the Rabbi in a study group on Judaism, Tuesday nights, 8:00 pm twice a month, Oct., Nov., Dec., beginning Oct 2nd
K.I. MITZVAH CORPS	I pledge to drive someone to the doctor, help deliver food after a death, visit someone in the hospital or other needed mitzvah

96

YOUR IDEAS

Did reading the stories make you think of:

• A project or program that some other congregation is doing, which might work in yours?
• Something entirely new?

Here's some space to jot down your ideas:

_____

_____

_____

_____

_____

_____

_____

_____

YOUR PREFERENCES

Among the ideas and stories, are there projects or programs which you think are especially appealing?

Here's space to list your preferences:

_____

_____

_____

_____

_____

_____

_____

_____

_____

_____

Insights into Outreach

**Practical perspectives
on important issues**

"The reward for the Mitzvah*
is the Mitzvah itself"
The Talmud

*good deed

Insights into Outreach

Clergy and lay people interviewed for this book were always eager to share insights about their projects and programs and also about the larger issues involved. When asked, "What do you think would be helpful for others to understand?" they were quick to respond, but they also frequently got going on the subject without even being asked.

Drawn mostly from the interviews, here are insights into such topics as faith and action, service and advocacy, band-aids and empowerment, risk and perseverance.

But do remember the fundamental point that was made so eloquently one beautiful Southern California afternoon by a lay-woman pioneer and mainstay of the outreach efforts of First Baptist Church in Fresno. The meeting with clergy and people from the congregation was about to end, and it was time for all to answer that all-important last question: What should others know about working with people in community service projects? Silence. Then, not nuts and bolts advice, but the answer that *should* have been expected but wasn't: "Just love them," she said.

Faith and action go hand in hand

Many clergy and lay people spoke of how faith and action go hand in hand, how faith was the reason for outreach involvement and how outreach, in turn, bolsters faith.

Perhaps the sign in front of Central Baptist in suburban Wayne, Pennsylvania, best sums up where many congregations active in outreach feel they are: "At the intersection of prayer and action"!

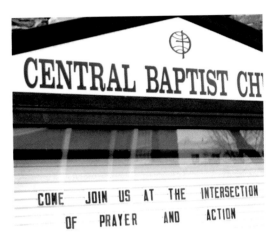

"True religion doesn't turn people out of the world, but helps them to live in it and excites them to mend it."

— Reverend Bill Stevens, First Friends Meeting, Greensboro, North Carolina, quoting William Penn

"The AME [African Methodist Episcopal] Church has a tradition of having the Bible in one hand and the newspaper in the other, and preaching from both; it's not a matter of just preaching from one, because you can get off balance. You have to have balance."

— Mark Whitlock, First AME Church, Los Angeles, California

"Our Lord has blessed us. We all worked together, everybody got a plot of land, each their own. Everything's working great, thank the lord!"

— Yolanda Martinez, Our Redeemer Lutheran Church, Livingston, California

"We couldn't just do bricks and mortar for ourselves with all that need out there."

— Reverend Rebecca Spencer, Central Congregational Church, Providence, Rhode Island

"We hear on Yom Kippur [the Jewish Day of Atonement], Isaiah 58, probably the most stirring challenge as to what it is God wants from us— it is not the sacrifices, but to house the homeless, feed the hungry, and clothe the naked. Every child sees people sleeping on the streets, and the challenge is not to let them ever get used to that, to think that's the way it is! . . . No matter what you take on, you're in there fighting for human dignity and for making life a little better and for infusing within your congregation that sense of duty, that you must do something!"

— Rabbi Robert Levine, Congregation Rodeph Sholom, New York, New York

"I go from one group to another, giving a talk on the sacraments, what does it mean to be a disciple, all these things, spending my time being a priest. They take that and turn it into . . . well, we should take care of the poor, and how are we going to do that? I find that here, when I am a priest, everything else falls into place . . . When the faith is authentic, they want to do something for someone else. We provide the space, and they find a way to do that."

— Father Joseph Justice (center in picture), Saint Anne Roman Catholic Church, Santa Ana, California

Doing outreach changes and satisfies people

When you reach out you gain a new understanding — about yourself, about conditions in society, and about other people that you may even have been afraid of. In turn, those you serve get to see the reality of caring people such as yourself.

The deep satisfaction felt by lay people in outreach is virtually universal. They feel they're acting out their faith, they're accomplishing something, they're helping someone else, they're making a difference and making the world a better place. Some say they have fun, and almost all say they receive more than they give. The conclusion: you're doing your congregation a real favor by encouraging outreach!

"I love the experience. If I could afford it I would do this all of the time, it's more than worth the effort. I'm not kidding when I tell the volunteers they're going to feel pretty good about themselves. I feel pretty good about myself. I'm a reasonably successful lawyer, but I have not gotten as much pleasure out of almost anything as I get out of this. One of the biggest kicks: I came into the Port Authority terminal late one night on a bus from the airport, and one of the guys who'd stayed at the shelter saw me and called out my name. I felt like a million dollars!"

— Jay Kranis, shelter coordinator, Congregation Rodeph Sholom, New York, New York

"They care about what they do. There's no guards; they trust us."

"You know, the way they treat us is Class A. We appreciate what they're doing for us."

— Two guests at the Rodeph Sholom shelter

"I'd always wanted to do volunteer work and to help out . . . You learn how to share with people who don't have as much . . . You learn not to be afraid of those people and to learn about their conditions because <u>you</u> could be in that position. God forbid, but you could. With some of these people that's how it happens: two or three bad things happen, and boom! All of a sudden, if you don't have family. . .

"I get something out of it myself. I think almost everybody does. You know you're helping people, partly so they don't have fear in their lives . . . I'd much rather they became independent . . . that's the highest form of charity and sometimes you can do it and sometimes you can't. I'm not helping them earn a living but I'm at least helping them not worry about their livelihood, about their own personal physical lives. They know this is a safe, secure place, and that's important.

"I always say if I ever won the lottery I'd travel and then I'd come back and do volunteer work. That's how you gain the most; you're giving the most back. I think people realize that there are people out there that need help and they can help them so easily. It requires minimal amounts of effort; I am major lazy, so if I can do this, anybody can do this.

"I'm trying to do my own bit — it's not that much but it's something. If everybody did something the world would be a better place. We all have to give of ourselves to help others. That's part of the lessons of Judaism, but that's also part of the lessons I was raised with by my parents . . . and you gain out of it, tremendous amounts."

— Dan Nichols, volunteer at the Rodeph Sholom shelter,
   New York, New York, but member of another temple

Outreach strengthens your congregation...and can make it grow!!!

Doing outreach creates a heightened sense of community, of taking part in a common endeavor. It results in stronger bonds among congregation members. Even when a good many people are not actively involved in a project, there frequently is a strong sense that "we are doing it." In addition to more diversity, vitality, renewed spirituality, and enthusiasm, congregations also frequently grow numerically.

Cutting edge projects can be a draw in themselves, often attracting previously unaffiliated people. All of which should be most heartening to readers in these days of mainline decline.

Some members of rapidly growing, outreach-oriented St. Mark's Episcopal Church, Corpus Cristi, Texas, participate in a run to raise money for the AIDS crisis (p. 41).

"Many people start as volunteers in our programs and then start coming to church because they can see what we are about. When people come here as visitors, they want to know, 'What are you doing to make a difference?' Turning outward alone leaves us burned out and empty, turning inward alone is just navel gazing. Both things have to work together."

— Reverend Sidney Skirvin, Church of the Pilgrims, Washington, D.C.

"This is not the same church that it was before all of this began; people have a tremendous pride and sense of purpose about what is being accomplished."

— Reverend Charles McCullough, First Church of Mission, Mission, Texas

"We've had people who joined the congregation, at least a dozen, who called up and joined because there was this little article about our partnership with the Abundance of Christ Church . . . We've had people not affiliated with a synagogue who said I can't believe a synagogue is doing this kind of thing, and it's so wonderful, and I want to be part of it!'

"Every religious institution is much more attractive to people when they feel it's 'walking its talk.' . . . What turns them on is when they see churches and synagogues that are actually rolling up their sleeves and getting involved in people's lives. It's the best PR for religion going."

— Rabbi Steven Carr Reuben, Congregation Kehillath Israel,
    Pacific Palisades, California

"In the last ten years we've had incredible growth. Predominantly that growth is the result of what people see us doing in the community; people come here because of what they see happening . . . We do a lot of risky things, I think without any question it has been a positive thing . . . People are saying, if I'm going to be part of a religious organization, that's the kind I'd like to be part of. So they come . . . I have realized that a person feels they are making a difference by being part of a congregation that's trying to make a difference, even though all they do is come to church. I didn't understand that some time ago. That's a big dynamic in this church, that 'I go to that place that's trying to change what's going on in society.'"

—Dr. George Regas, rector of All Saints Church Episcopal Church,
    Pasadena, California

Outreach begets outreach . . . and more!

Doing outreach tends to snowball: a first effort often leads to more, and a congregation with several things going may find still others surfacing as enthusiasm builds. Making a first project a success is extremely important: try to pick a winner if you want to get outreach really going in your congregation.

A bonus: successful fundraising for outreach may generate a generous spirit that makes non-outreach projects happen, too. For example, the year they did their Habitat house, First Friends also successfully funded its handicap access improvements, driveway and covered entrance.

"Outreach is infectious; once people get involved, they begin to influence the whole church to keep looking for more ways to help."
— Sister Lorraine Menheer, St. Ann's Parish, Barrington, Illinois

The Seeds of Hope project started by Washington Street United Methodist Church in Columbia, South Carolina (p. 61) spread not just to other congregations in South Carolina but as far as New York City.

Your example really counts

Your congregation can serve as a model for others when you address a clear need that's not being met. For instance, you might be the first church or synagogue in your area to tackle AIDS or drugs, or to set up an after-school program or do a joint project with a congregation of another denomination or faith.

Your example of being open and inclusive and doing things to love your neighbors can extend even further, into the workplace and the lives of the people of your congregation, and beyond your congregation as well. The *Outreach Beyond Outreach* section of this book explores this further.

Key Benefits of Outreach

Accomplishments. You do something, you make a difference!

Individual Satisfaction. There's nothing that can beat living your faith, "walking your talk."

Better Understanding, Personal Growth and Change. Outreach can bring you face to face with "them" and with the stereotypes you may have formed. You gain an understanding of people and their problems and potentials and aspirations, and of their communities. And working with others can significantly improve understanding and respect among races, denominations and faiths.

Congregational Revitalization. Outreach brings congregations to life, rekindling the spirit of their faith community.

Congregational Growth. Over and over, people in congregations active in outreach re-echo this fact: outreach makes that church or synagogue attractive to people who want to "make a difference." New people will join, present members will stay, former members will rejoin a congregation that is committed to acting out its faith.

Spin-offs. Your example is extremely important. Your outreach efforts can inspire similar efforts by others — other congregations, organizations, businesses, even government.

Focus your efforts on the needs

What you do, and where, will be among the toughest choices you will make. Appalachia, abroad, your own community, your immediate neighborhood, your own congregation, the inner city, another part of the metropolitan area, downstate — the possibilities may seem endless.

Possibly there will be severe needs right on your doorstep and, as is the case of St. Paul's in Philadelphia which supports the Cunningham Community Center, you may be the only game in town. If you're in an affluent area or far from the problems, what and where can be key questions in your outreach decisions. In any community you can find needs to address, but if you have limited resources is that where you should commit them?

As Reverend Stephen Jones of Central Baptist in Wayne, Pennsylvania, says, "Anybody who thinks the suburbs don't have problems is wrong . . . nonetheless, the intensity is not the same." So it may come down to being a question of the severity of the need. Even if you could do it, whatever it is, in your own community, is that the right place? Where is the greater need? If you don't meet the need, who will? All Saints, in Pasadena, 25 miles from downtown Los Angeles, teamed up with a Los Angeles synagogue to rehabilitate skid row housing in downtown L.A. — because they simply felt that's where the greatest need was.

All Saints' efforts include: top: rehabilitating a former "skid row" hotel in downtown Los Angeles (p. 67), and above: starting the Union Station homeless shelter in Pasadena, where the church is located.

For larger or more active congregations, the answer may be to do more than one thing: All Saints also addresses needs in its own community. But if you feel you can make just one effort you, you will want to consider very carefully where and what you pick.

Outreach and inreach go together

"Making a difference" can mean going outside your congregation, to meet needs in the community or beyond. But it can also mean focusing on very real needs within your congregation. An example is a job search support program for your congregation's out-of-work members.

Inreach can also be crucial to doing outreach; indeed, "heal thyself" is a vital concept, in that it empowers your own people. In practical terms, people in your congregation who are out of work may lack the psychological stamina, physical energy or financial resources to work with others on their problems.

Church of the Risen Savior in Albuquerque, New Mexico, began a mental health support group for members of their own congregation. It quickly expanded to include the community at large (p.37).

Inreach can be powerful other ways. It can draw in some of the many congregation members who may not yet have been involved either in inreach or outreach, and it can set an example for still others. In this way, inreach can be both a learning experience and a demonstration of how to respond to others' needs through a congregational effort.

Finally, the very act of helping and loving each other in your own religious community can enable your people to understand a problem and stimulate them to love a more distant neighbor.

Service gives authenticity to social action: the service/advocacy pyramid

A strong advocate for change needs to truly understand the problems and how people are affected by them.

Many congregations find that their service work, such as running a shelter, is necessary as a base for their advocacy and social action work and leads naturally to it. Thinking of this as a pyramid with service as a base, is helpful.

ADVOCACY

SERVICE

"We have a pyramid that we work with: social service or outreach at the broad base of that pyramid. Then social education, social witness, and social action. In many liberal churches this pyramid has been on its head; it's been on its point. Social witness or action is deemed to be the only truly revolutionary and therefore honorable road to follow for a church. Unfortunately, what happens is that a pyramid placed on its point is intrinsically unstable. Churches end up dividing within themselves over, for instance, whether they're more against war than hunger...

What we do is build our pyramid on the broad base of social outreach which is—regardless of one's politics, regardless of one's specific beliefs— a universal. It divides no one. Everyone can take part. Then the social education comes, which helps us to understand better the nature of the problems ... And then as we become more passionately committed, more active, more informed, there are opportunities for witness, such as in marching or writing Congress people and even the possibility for action, but it comes out of the experience of those moments when the church has a basis of knowledge, experience, familiarity that gives an authority to the action or the witness that we otherwise might not have."

— Reverend Forrester Church, Unitarian Church of All Souls, New York, New York

"Band-aids" are valid, but the concept is changing

As the Chinese proverb goes, "Give someone a fish and you feed them for a day; teach someone to fish and you feed them for a lifetime." There's no question that we should help people learn to fish; if at all possible we should not start and stop with the hand-out. Many who run soup kitchens and shelters agree: they try to provide or refer people to as much counseling and other assistance as possible towards independence.

But the basics of the band-aid are also vitally important: people can't learn to fish on an empty stomach.

"Without the band-aid, the wound never heals. . .you have to have the band-aid so healing can take place. . . .

"Our guests, they come here, no questions asked, no qualifications. We offer them a hot nutritious meal designed to sustain them for 24 hours . . . and then we have the legal action center for the homeless, a medical van . . . A counseling/referrals program offers guests a place to talk, a place to be heard, a place where they can get referrals to meet the myriad needs they have.

"All of those things are band-aids, but they're steps forward. The food is the first band-aid, just as the shelter is the first band-aid. People who participate in our counseling and referrals program . . . they're not required to do this. The fact that they are willing to take that first step, for whatever the motivation, brings them one step closer to the things that they need to improve their lives today and to take steps forward for more productive lives tomorrow. All that's under that band-aid."

— Kami O'Keefe, Director of Development, Church of the Holy
   Apostles, New York, New York

Suburbs and cities working together is vitally important

Fifty years ago the great majority of people in metropolitan areas lived in the central cities. Today, most live in the suburbs.

With urban problems severe and growing worse, there is an urgent need for the time, talent and treasure now concentrated in suburban congregations to be brought to bear on meeting inner city needs.

Many suburban churches feel they should be doing things in the central city, and a growing number are, sometimes pairing with an inner city congregation. Other partnerships can be formed with schools, city government, central city development corporations, coalitions of congregations, businesses and others.

Second Grace United Methodist Church, Detroit, Michigan, formed a partnership with First United Methodist Church in the suburbs to adopt this city school, making a huge difference to its students (p. 47).

There are also organizations like Boston's 177-year-old City Mission Society which engage in advocacy and offer volunteer opportunities as well as staffed service programs, all focused on working with the urban poor to bring about change. Much of City Mission's work would not be possible without continuing support from suburban congregations.

A fundamental challenge in working with a city, as one suburban minister put it, is: "How does a suburban church be in partnership with a city in ways that are not paternalistic, so that we don't show up and say 'we've got all the money, all the ideas, here's what's good for you?'"

You will find some examples of partnerships in this book and more by researching your own area; also see the *Outreach Beyond Outreach* section.

Hancock Congregational (UCC) Church, Lexington, Massachusetts, is among many suburban churches involved with City Mission Society of Boston.

Hands-on doesn't always win over check writing

Direct service projects can accomplish enormous amounts and can really motivate a congregation to do outreach.

Hands-on projects are favored by many congregations for three reasons. First, they're often less expensive, with free volunteer time being substituted for paid services. Secondly, for most people there's nothing like direct involvement for the feeling of satisfaction in having accomplished something and in knowing they are acting out their faith.

Finally, many congregations recognize that direct participation in a service project — for example, working with the homeless or doing literacy training — helps people understand those they're working with — and vice-versa.

Some of the inner city loans made by Philadelphia's United Bank are made possible by deposits from members of suburban congregations such as Central Baptist (p. 93).

But in some cases, money <u>is</u> the answer. For example, building homes and helping people start new businesses depend on capital. If you think of capital as transferable power, a congregation that writes a check may be doing something quite powerful, and quite beyond anything else it could do, by providing a form of assistance that may be unavailable from any other source.

The same thing can be said about providing financial support to your denomination's outreach activities.

To get people's commitment, there must be a mutual understanding of needs

People will give you both their time and their commitment, if they understand your needs and you understand theirs.

Your educational efforts are key to drawing people in: when they understand a problem, and what they can do about it, they are likely to come forward and join the effort. If your activity meets their needs, you may even attract new members to your congregation.

Many people, however, will actually participate only if you ask for a well defined and limited commitment — most have busy, full lives with obligations they can't neglect, such as work and family.

Some people may be willing to make a much greater commitment or can be more flexible, but even people who you might think would have a lot of time, such as retired folks, may well have many other interests and commitments.

But be sure to ask: people do want to be involved.

"I do believe that people participate in things that they get satisfaction out of; they don't participate if they don't get satisfaction, no matter how lofty their ideals may be. If they aren't getting anything out of it, emotionally, spiritually, or whatever, then they drop out. Things that work are the things where people go somewhere, they have a hands-on sense of helping people or being involved with people and interacting with people. . . Try not to expect people to make long-term commitments; unfortunate, but that's how it works."

— Rabbi Steven Carr Reuben, Kehillath Israel,
   Pacific Palisades, California

"When I first came to town I went to another church and then I just stopped going to church, I didn't like organized religion. And then I began to have friends that had AIDS or were HIV-positive and I thought, I can't do this, so then I thought, I'll join a church, you kind of get desperate, you think of just anything. My next-door neighbor mentioned going to church . . . and said come and visit . . . This church had this education program and I visited several times and it was almost like I kind of felt that I needed to do things to make myself all right . . . I became involved almost for a selfish reason. I had to do something for me or I was just going to go crazy. On my own I wasn't this real aggressive person who would have gone out and done something, but the church started it, and I thought, 'This is easy, I can get into this, it's there for me.' And it was for that reason I stayed at this church. If I had gone in and there hadn't been anything, I am sure that I would have eventually left because at that point that's what I was looking for and I need to become involved and I need to be doing something because I can't stop this disease, which is what I want to do, but I can do something about it."

— A church AIDS volunteer

"The key in any large institution, including a church, is getting people involved. You've got to have them involved more than Sunday mornings, or else they can just be overwhelmed by the place. They don't look upon this as just a place where they're going to have an Episcopal service. We give all sorts of opportunities and publicize as widely as we can . . . On a Sunday, before and after the service, we have open air presentations of different things, groups, ways in which people can do things and get to know people . . . Get a person into a small group and they begin to get friends and get a feeling that they can belong here . . . Many do modest acts and feel very good about what they do if even in a small way."

— Russ Kully, All Saints Episcopal Church, Pasadena, California

Recognize the power of one or two "sparkplugs"

"It's impossible to overemphasize the importance of one or two people who want something to start and who can and will devote significant time, energy, and care to making it happen. This is often the catalyst that makes it possible for a congregation to begin to use a treasure house of latent resources and talents."

— Bill Holshouser, Old Cambridge Baptist Church, Cambridge, Massachusetts

Recognize the power of spiritual energy . . . . . and the need to refuel

Some outreach programs can be very taxing. Working on difficult problems in difficult surroundings, scaring up resources to make things happen, keeping others enthused — all this can make "burnout" a risk for even the most dedicated of volunteers. And with burnout comes falling away, and weakening of the project.

A firm, spiritual commitment from the start, with people discerning the project as a call to which they are responding, is a major key to success. As a denominational staff person put it, "We have to listen to God's Spirit: where do we sense God/Yahweh is calling us to be?"

For an ongoing project, one Massachusetts clergywoman has found that periodic refueling of spiritual energy can make all the difference, for instance by gathering all the volunteers in a worship service once a month to share problems and frustrations — and joys — with one another.

Hiring paid staff may be a necessity

Volunteer projects can provide wonderful opportunities for members of your congregation, and using only volunteers can keep costs down. However, hiring paid staff may be necessary for the success of a program because of its complexity or the need for professionally trained people.

While hiring staff means raising more money, it can also support your arguments that your program will be well managed and therefore is deserving of financial support.

Seniors program director, Carol Shissler, of Cass Community United Methodist Church in Detroit, Michigan (p. 28).

John Palaylay, director of East San Diego Presbyterian's after-school program (p.46).

Mary Vradelis (r) and her assistant Lakeesha Gage. Lakeesha is a student in the Back-on-Track program that Mary directs for Third Baptist Church and Temple Emanu-El in San Francisco (p.45).

Worried about money? ASK: you may be amazed at the response

If you can make a compelling case for your project, people will give. But be sure to *say* you need their contribution; sales people call it "asking for the sale." And don't ask for too little — let *them* say, "I won't give you ten but I'll give you five." Lots of small gifts can make big things happen.

If your congregation includes people with substantial or even moderate wealth, they may expect to be asked: they know they have the resources to make a real difference. As one minister said: "They expect it of me. I take them out to lunch and make the case, and I ask them. And sometimes they'll write out a check right there. And I've had more than one say, handing me the check, 'Is that enough?' So don't underestimate their generosity!"

Finally, you may not know people's wealth, so even ask those you may think have little — you may be surprised.

All this, of course, goes for non-financial contributions as well, such as materials or services: be sure to ask.

"We have all the levels of economic status and we've had a lot of problems recently with people without work. But there's never been a need, in these 25 years that I've been here, that I couldn't pick up a telephone to fulfill. The gifts are there; the gifts are always there. People are so willing to give; they just want to be asked."

— Wilda Babineaux, St. Jules Catholic Church,
   Lafayette, Louisiana

"There's a lot of untapped resources. You just don't know . . . but if you grab someone's interest, and that's what's so important . . . you don't know what people are willing to give if they get pulled into something."

— Mary Lou Tietz, Associate Director of Family Life Services,
   First Trinity Lutheran Church, Washington, D.C.

Partnerships can be worth the trouble. . . and a lot of fun!

Whether or not you're dealing with urban/suburban relationships, you will find that some things either can't be done alone or are better done in partnership — with one or more congregations or organizations. Having a partner increases the number of people and the amount of financial and other resources available. It can also boost enthusiasm and give the project added purpose and credibility to help sustain it. Doing something together also enables people to get to know and understand one another, as well as to achieve the primary goals of the project. People with joint church/synagogue projects remark on how this always happens.

The costs? Probably more coordination, meetings — but less in terms of outlay. Depending on the project, you may want to limit the number of partners.

"Working with the temple has gotten intriguing. First it was just the Habitat house, and then the idea of the connections—how else would we get together and sing songs? He plays his guitar and we sing Jewish songs and Christian songs."

— Reverend Woody Carlson, Holy Trinity Lutheran, Church
   Seattle, Washington

"The best advice is to do it with another congregation because it's not only fun that way but it cuts the cost in half. It all of a sudden becomes very manageable . . . but you wouldn't want too many congregations. One other has been very manageable."

—Marta Hurwitz, Congregation B'nai Torah, which worked with
   Holy Trinity Lutheran on a Habitat for Humanity House,
   Seattle, Washington

Trust your vision: persistence pays

In your outreach efforts you may be doing things you weren't trained to do, going through uncharted waters, and there will be some rough going. But don't let it get to you. Unless your vision is flawed — in which case you should re-think it and modify it as necessary — there's every reason to hang in there, be persistent. The Our Redeemer story on p. 60 is an excellent example of the ultimate success which persistence and resourcefulness can bring.

"You don't learn this stuff in seminary at all! They threw me in the water and I had to learn how to swim . . . It's all been a learning experience, and we're just looking for the right equation. It will come together because the idea is good. There are enough people in the community who won't let it drop."

— Reverend Bill Ruth, Our Redeemer Lutheran Church, Livingston, California, quoted before the land for the community farm was found.

The land that became a successful community farm was the **fourth** *site attempted.*

Recognize failure as a real possibility

If you talk to other congregations, you're sure to find projects and programs that did not succeed. Rather than reject such a project entirely, learn from their experience. Find out why it failed, and then see if it was basically an unworkable idea or one that can be modified to work for you.

An important thing to be able to recognize is when a project really isn't a good choice for your congregation: it may be a great idea, but you don't have the resources and are unlikely to be able to get them, or there's just not a good fit with your interests, or another organization is a natural to do it.

A complex housing rehabilitation project is a good example of something that might be out of reach for a smaller congregation without any experience. At the same time, that congregation could give such a project a boost, for example by pointing out the possibility to another organization or by helping to fund it through a community development loan fund.

ITEM: In the East, a church bought and partially rehabilitated an apartment building but ended up being sued by tenants for code violations it was unable to correct. The problem: inadequate financial resources to start with, coupled with a downturn in the economy which meant loss of tenants and income as people lost their jobs and moved out. So the church didn't have enough cash flow to complete the renovation of the building.

ITEM: In the Midwest, a church-sponsored restaurant was started to create jobs, a more modest, storefront version of the 3rd & Eats restaurant on p. 57. It had great food, a lot of enthusiasm, and everything seemed to be going for it. But it failed — because of a business miscalculation: it was in the wrong location. There just weren't enough customers to keep the doors open.

THE MORAL: Make sure you have a basically sound idea, and plan your project or program carefully.

Taking risks is fundamental to outreach

While genuine risk assessment is good to do, and the possibility of failure is real, outreach just isn't the place for ultra-conservative risk management and too cautious an approach.

Reaching out by its very nature is something of a risk, and if you're acting out your faith, risking is part and parcel of it. After all, did Jesus stay away from the woman who was being stoned, for fear the stones might be hurled at him? Or did Moses refuse to lead his people, saying "Maybe we won't get to the promised land, so let's not try?"

So, you will always want to consider these two fundamental questions:

• What are we risking by *not* going ahead with this project? Balanced against the risk of failure is the chance of success!

• If *we* don't take the risk, who will?

Actually, in many cases, you may be risking very little. In dollar terms, since you are dealing with your community's collective resources, the risk may not amount to much on an individual basis. For instance, a 200-member congregation that risks $10,000 to start something — that's just $50 each. Doing this kind of financial analysis, you may find yourselves able to do things as a congregation that members would never do as individuals.

If you think of your non-monetary resources such as volunteer time or the use of your building as "soft" capital that's expendable, there's really no risk there. Finally, if you take a risky social action or advocacy position and lose part of your congregation, you may well find that replacements soon join because they are attracted by your willingness to stand up for your beliefs.

There may be real risk, however, in terms of substantial liability. To protect yourself, you can get liability insurance or incorporate a program as a separate entity, as do many congregations that are involved in such activities as day care or development.

Secondly, running a test is a good idea, if your project lends itself to that. Temple Emanu-El and Third Baptist in San Francisco had a three-month trial of their highly successful after-school program before hiring staff. The volunteer coordinators provided feedback on how things were working, what went well and what didn't, and there was also a chance to see how enthusiastic the partner congregations would be.

Beware: Always look out for the naysayers who aren't doing real risk assessment but are just against anything new. It won't work or may not work, they say, or it won't make a difference, or it will get in the way of something else our church or synagogue is doing. Don't let them get in the way of what you *know* you should be doing!

Temple Emanu-El and Third Baptist in San Francisco had a three-month trial of their highly successful after-school program before hiring staff.

"*Almost every religious institution on some level or other is struggling, and there's a natural inclination within an institution, as within our own lives, to say, I've got to be very careful. If you want to use a metaphor for this, my cup is only half full and I've got to be very careful not to spill anything in it. What happens is that the water slowly evaporates. You don't spill anything. The biblical challenge to that is to empty your cup and be filled, and so you pour it out and your cup is all of a sudden overflowing. It's only when you dare to risk that action that the Holy Spirit kicks in, and the loaves and fishes start multiplying. But for the person who's afraid of spilling the cup, it just evaporates!*"

— Reverend Forrester Church, Unitarian Church of All Souls
  New York, New York

Congregations alone can't solve
all the problems . . .

Many people interviewed, especially those dealing with enormous, seemingly intractable inner city problems, spoke passionately of the need for major resources and a change of priorities.

"I would never want to call it a permanent operation. It's temporary but it's open-ended in terms of how temporary the problem of hunger in our midst is. . . someday we'd like to close the doors of Holy Apostles' soup kitchen because the problem has been dealt with, not because we're burned out, run out of money, lost the will . . .

". . . For the vast bulk of people we serve, it's mind-boggling what it would take to put a life back together in a significant way that we would recognize as acceptable . . . The problems, all of them are labor-intensive, costly . . . For instance, we have people who want to go into drug-rehab. They ought to be able to go — just like that!

". . . I despair about our country until there's a national political will to address these problems with the money, the resources, the brains, the manpower, as an urgent matter of national defense. We are a bare-bones operation, keeping people alive until there's something better . . .

". . . We go to the entire New York metropolitan area to raise our funds; if we had thousands of churches trying to raise the money, we couldn't do it. To get more churches to replicate what we're doing would not be an answer because we'd be in competition for the same scarce dollars. That's the rub there. The only place the money can finally come from, if we're going to substantively deal with the issues of America, is the federal government—that's the only place. That's why everything is a holding operation until this country changes its attitudes and priorities.

"These are God's children . . . if I didn't have the religious perspective that gives me a sense of the significance of what we're doing, I would have given up, gone crazy, hit my head against the wall and gone screaming into the night long ago. But there is that religious dimension that alone holds us together."

— Reverend William Greenlaw, rector of Church of the Holy
   Apostles, New York, New York

. . . but if every congregation pitched in, what a difference we could make!

Whether it was clergy or volunteers speaking, that wondering "what if we all did something. . ." came up over and over again in conversations with people in every denomination and faith, all across the country.

The sampling of stories in this book shows there's always *something* that a congregation can do to make a difference. With more than 300,000 congregations nationwide doing something, or something extra, what enormous changes we could make!

So, it's time to take a look at how to decide on a "something" and how to "make it happen" — in your congregation.

"Paul says, I can do all things through Christ, who strengthens me— what is there that God's church can't do? There's nothing in this world we can't do! So let's get on and do it—intelligently, of course; you can't do it on inspiration and you can't do it on perspiration. You've got to do it on inspiration and perspiration, mind working, body working, soul working!"

— Reverend Cecil Murray, pastor of First AME Church, Los Angeles, California

Getting Things to Happen

**Making outreach
a reality in your
congregation**

"Whatever you can do, or dream you can, begin it: boldness has genius, power and magic in it."

Johann Wolfgang von Goethe

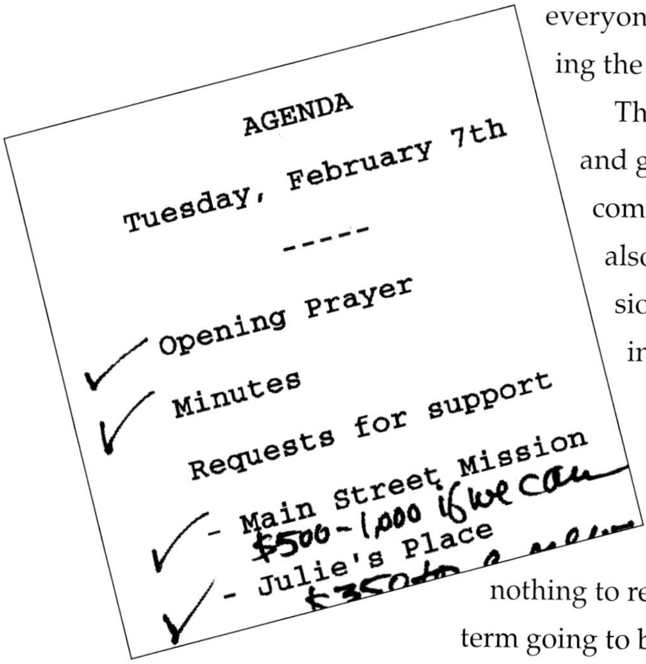

You may know this scene quite well: It's a Tuesday evening. Outreach Committee people have arrived for the monthly meeting they've become accustomed to: a handful of well intentioned folks from the congregation, all adults, everyone pretty much on time, a few missing, the chair calling the meeting to order, a prayer, reviewing the minutes.

Then, down to business: by and large, how to evaluate and get the money to respond to requests received from community organizations, how to respond to them and also faithfully to the denomination, etc. On an occasional Tuesday there's a guest from an agency, pleading their case.

Most of the time there's nothing initiated, nothing "hands on", nothing involving either the committee or the congregation in a proactive role. Not much spark, not much to get excited about, and nothing to really prevent some from wondering, "*When* is my term going to be over?" Yet they hang in there, knowing that doing outreach is part and parcel of being a responsible congregation, and *they're* the ones who have volunteered to do it.

When they're through with the half dozen or so meetings over the course of the year, they *can* point to some accomplishments: they've supported a number of social service agencies and other organizations in the community and at the national level. They've

AGENDA

Tuesday, February 7th

✓ Opening Prayer

✓ Minutes

Requests for support

✓ - Main Street Mission
   $500 - 1,000 if we can

✓ - Julie's Place
   $350...

kept up their reputation as a congregation that does a lot of outreach, at least as compared to many others. Yet, for some there's
this feeling they haven't done much after all. And certainly it
wasn't very satisfying. And certainly they've hardly tapped the
resources of the congregation.

The exception was when someone in the congregation, either
on the committee or off, sailed in with a pet project and made it
fly: setting up a refugee family in an apartment in town, or getting
some of the folks in the congregation to volunteer at a soup
kitchen in an adjacent community.

Sound familiar? Maybe not, if yours is one of the congregations where not much is going on or where the pet
project meteor never flashes across your outreach sky.
On the other hand, it's possibly not an accurate picture because
yours is one of the many congregations all over the country where
outreach *is* really exciting — lots of people are involved, and
there's a feeling of solid accomplishment.

Hopefully what follows will help you to get things to happen
in your congregation, maybe for the first time, or enable you to do
outreach even more effectively.

The process described applies
best to the committee centered
style of doing outreach (see the
next page), but much of it will also
be useful in other styles of doing
things.

Obviously, feel free to modify
the steps suggested here; there's
certainly no single right way to get
a project to GO!

*Congregational Church of Weston out-
reach committee meets with SHARE
New England representative to learn
about starting a SHARE program.*

STYLE

What's your style?

Congregations often have a style of doing outreach. There seem to be three basic ones:

• **Strong Pastoral or Staff Leadership**
The outreach activity is suggested, strongly supported or propelled by the vision and determination of clergy or staff.

• **Committee Centered**
An "outreach committee" does most of the research, decision making, planning and executing, or sets up sub-groups to do it.

• **Entrepreneurial**
A person or a group comes up with its own agenda and plan and even fundraisers, builds its support constituency, and independently goes ahead and "does its own thing." A congregation may contain many such outreach groups.

Sometimes the styles are a bit mixed: initially, for instance, there is a strong clergy lead, but the ball is quickly picked up by lay leaders and pursued without very much further clergy involvement.

In your own congregation, choice of style may depend on what just feels comfortable, how large your congregation is, and the nature of your projects. But style really doesn't matter, as long as you *do* things.

and LEADERSHIP

Spark plugs, champions, and key leaders

Whichever your style and whatever your project, invariably there will be three key "people" forces at work if you are going to succeed.

• **The Spark Plug**
This is another name for the entrepreneur, the enthusiastic person who may have had the idea in the first place, and is certainly the driving force behind making the project or activity a reality.

• **The Champion**
This may be clergy, an influential member of the congregation, or a group vitally interested in seeing the project happen. The support of the champion is especially important at crucial times, such as when a vote is needed or funding is requested.

• **Key Leaders**
Especially if the project is complex, dedicated and capable leaders will be needed to organize and manage the practical side of the project and make sure all cylinders are firing.

For success in your efforts, you'll be wise to give the spark plugs a chance to make their sparks; recognize, encourage, and support the champions; and identify and recruit the best leaders you can find!

GET PEOPLE INVOLVED

Get people excited, seeing possibilities

This book is meant to get you enthused about outreach, to see it as an opportunity — as well as a responsibility — for your congregation.

If you can pass that enthusiasm along to others, the outreach potential of your congregation can really come alive. Additional copies of this book may be a big help, perhaps for all outreach committee members, interested clergy and key lay leaders

Meetings and retreats, events and programs to share ideas and enthusiasm, coupled with an openness to outreach ideas and involvement from all comers — all these can really light the fire!

Some of the people involved in the AIDS outreach efforts of Christ Episcopal Church in Raleigh, North Carolina.

Sayville Congregational Church, NY, held an outreach retreat facilitated by its former interim minister (not pictured here) who knew the group but had no stake in the outcome (a decision to do a housing project in the community).

Stay open, inclusive: welcome people's ideas

Especially at the beginning, when you're trying to define a direction for your outreach efforts, consider inviting the whole congregation to participate. The more you can get people interested from the beginning, the easier it will be to keep them involved later on.

An all-are-welcome outreach retreat with a good facilitator, or a series of meetings can be a good way to begin. You may find that some very interesting ideas will emerge, unknown skills will surface, and people who were thought not to be interested will actually volunteer.

It's also an excellent way to identify the key lay people you will need: if you let people know you're open to their ideas, it's probable that those who make suggestions become the project's key people. Indeed, in congregations which use the "entrepreneurial" approach, the committed leadership almost always surfaces, along with the things they want to do.

Important: Many projects start, and some continue for all their active lives, with small "mission groups" rather than the whole congregation. While full congregational involvement may be desirable, often it just doesn't happen, and all possible encouragement should be given to the small group that is ahead of the congregation in recognizing a problem and doing something about it.

Focus on discerning a call

If your outreach effort is to be truly an expression of your faith, you should be focusing on discerning a real call: what do you perceive is a truly faithful way, at this time, to respond to God's will? Spiritual guidance from your own clergy or from others skilled in this discernment process can be crucial to the power of your outreach and its ability to be sustained.

CHECK THINGS OUT

Check your horizons

What you do, and where, has a lot to do with what you see as your service area or interest area. Try drawing a rough diagram or two, perhaps using a map, with your neighborhood as the center.

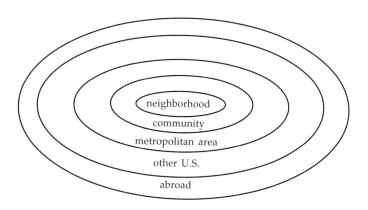

neighborhood
community
metropolitan area
other U.S.
abroad

What and where are the needs?

Especially if you're in an inner city, some of the needs may be ultra clear, virtually on your doorstep. Even in such a case, selecting a focus will help you understand the range of needs you might meet.

You can get information for an initial "needs assessment" from your own knowledge, from a survey you do, and from published material. Doing this study is an excellent job for someone who enjoys research.

Talk with experts in your area, such as community development staff and city planners, teachers and school staff, social service agency workers, and community leaders. Also ask which needs they think are the most serious. Don't forget the experts in your own congregation!

Your denomination's local office or an ecumenical organization may have done a survey or know of one and could offer insights. For needs beyond your area, contact your denomination or other organizations.

Important: Be sure to talk directly with the people you might be serving, to fully understand their perspectives, priorities and aspirations and to see how best to work together as partners to bring about results that truly meet their needs.

Pawtucket Congregational Church in Rhode Island had a student ask community leaders and others about needs, which led to the church's shelter project.

Find out what's happening

There may be a lot of things already going on, or planned, to address the needs you see or hear of. By finding out what these are, you can avoid duplicating efforts and get a better handle on unmet needs. You may also find programs that you can hook into or use as models.

By touring local programs and talking with people, you can gain insights into how programs work: for instance, what a homeless shelter looks like from the inside, or how an after-school program operates.

If someone can put together a tour of programs in your area, you can see a variety of types of projects in a short time. You might want to arrange this as a joint effort with people from other congregations.

Remember to talk with ecumenical and denomination staff about the programs they know of.

Members of suburban congregations take a bus tour to find out how the Boston Community Loan Fund works.

SIZE UP YOUR RESOURCES

Find out your congregation's skills and interests

Perhaps your most important resource is your own members. Most congregations have a great wealth of "people" assets: members who have skills, interests and connections that can make outreach a reality. Yet those assets may be largely hidden, as there usually is little information about what members can and, very important, *wan*t to do.

To find out more about your members, you can use an informal approach: just chat with them and make some notes. Or, you can use a questionnaire like the one on p. 143. Then create a talents/skills/interests/connections file, perhaps on a computer, so you can tap into this major resource as needed.

Important: If you ask people what they'd like to do, be sure to follow up with an offer to help find an outlet for those interests or a promise to keep them in mind for the future.

First Friends in North Carolina found right in their congregation of 250 all but one of the skills necessary to build this Habitat house (they hired someone to finish the sheet rock).

The town of Fairfield, Connecticut made its old police headquarters available as a community-wide shelter.

St. Timothy's, Norwood, Massachusetts uses its beautiful lakefront site for a picnic for city shelter residents and staff.

How about other resources?

There are many resources that you either have already or may be able to get to support outreach efforts.

Your **congregation** has not only its own members but many other assets as well: staff, endowments or other financial resources, buildings, land, even your parking lot. Your location can be a major asset. A potential partner congregation can offer the same.

Your **community** also has resources you can tap into: public land and buildings; goods, services, time and financial contributions that individuals and businesses can offer; financial support from foundations; nonprofit organizations' staff services and the use of their facilities.

Your **denomination** may have: experts to help with program development and training in organization and leadership; work camps and other programs both overseas and at home; and possibly funds to support your efforts.

You can use the checklist on p. 144 to list resources you identify.

CHOOSE YOUR FOCUS

Select needs you want to address

From your needs survey, you will have a list of the kinds of needs that are out there. Which of these seem appealing to you? Which ones do you think you could tackle in some way?

Making a selection will require your taking a look at your present and potential resources and the interests and skills of your own people.

Your selection may also be shaped by your answers to the questions below; the *Insights* section may be helpful, too. You can use the checklist on p. 145 to list the top needs you might address.

St. Paul's in Philadelphia, Pennsylvania, has focused on its own neighborhood and the community center right next to the church.

Holy Apostles, New York, New York, concentrates mainly on one thing: its massive soup kitchen and assistance program.

Focus Questions

What are your preferences? Check or circle them.

• Next door, elsewhere in area, out of state, or abroad?

• Hands-on or not?

• Inreach or outreach?

• Service, social action or advocacy?

• Alone or with a partner?

• One-shot or continuing?

• One thing or many?

• Something new, or expansion of what we do now?

• Do it; start it then "spin it off"; set it up as something separate from the start?

• No-cost/low-cost, or substantial funding?

By building and shipping tractors, Summit Chapel, Johnstown, Pennsylvania, chose to address poor farmers' needs in Central America, without going there.

NARROW THINGS DOWN

Pick three potential projects

Make a first cut: list three potential outreach projects or activities. They can be from this book, things you've heard about or seen elsewhere, or things you just dream up. Write them on the checklist on p. 147.

Be as specific as you can as to who, what, where and when. For example, a suburban church might make a list like the one at the right:

• Our congregation to develop a counseling and job-finding program with an inner city church to start in the fall.

• Our congregation, all ages, to fund and build, hands on, a Habitat house this spring.

• Our teenagers to go on a youth work camp trip this summer in the U.S.A. or overseas.

WANTED:
Suburban church wants inner city church as partner in setting up a counseling/job-finding service for benefit of out-of-work people in inner city church's congregation/neighborhood.

Identify potential partners

You may want to have another congregation as a partner — to boost the resources available to carry it out, or for other reasons such as developing inner city/suburban ties or for strengthening interfaith or interdenominational relationships. Some projects will actually require a partner.

Use your own network to find potential partners, or ask your clergy council, denomination or an ecumenical organization for some suggestions. If you think of it as a personal ad or bulletin board poster, it may help you to define the offer.

Other kinds of partners, and most important ones, are foundations or businesses or local government that will underwrite your efforts or make in-kind contributions of staff, facilities, goods or services. A social service agency or your denomination are other important potential partners.

Make a tentative choice

For each potential project ask: Would this project:
- Satisfy a real need (i.e., really make a difference)?
- Be something our members would like to do?
- Fit with our "focus" preferences (see p. 146)?
- Be possible with present or likely resources?
- Serve a need greater than the other potential projects?
- Serve any of our congregation's own needs (see p. 145)?

Then make a tentative choice.

Rough out a broad plan

The checklist on p. 148 gives the framework for a plan and the major elements you need to include.

VISIT AND/OR SPEAK WITH PEOPLE DOING IT

Find out still more

By the time you've gotten to this point, it's time to find out more in order to make a detailed plan and decide if it's a go situation.

If you haven't already done so, invite people to come and talk with you. Even better, and this point cannot be overemphasized, *go and visit a similar program/project and see the activity in action*. Nothing beats actually being there and asking people questions face to face!

The people involved in the projects in this book are good sources (the churches and synagogues are listed in the *Resources* section), but it would be even better if you can find a similar project nearby. That would give you a place you could easily visit, and more than just once. Your denominational office or the ecumenical agencies and other organizations listed in the *Resources* section are good places to call to identify projects and programs near you (even a 100-mile trip is nearby). Programs such as SHARE have staff that can pinpoint programs in your area and provide pointers, materials and training.

CHECKING IT OUT. . .

Here's how one outreach committee investigated doing SHARE, (p. 19) which had been recommended to their chair by the associate minister for outreach of their denomination's state conference.

top: A SHARE staffer explains the program to the committee at their church. top right: Visiting the SHARE warehouse. left: Visiting the coordinator of a congregation near their own which runs a program. right: Their own program, undertaken just two months later, is a success!

MAKE YOUR CHOICE

Re-check your decision...

Check your objectives and your resources once again. Do you really have, or can you get, everything necessary to make your project fly — the people, funds, facilities? Will they enable this to be an ongoing activity, if that's your objective? What's the risk, and are you willing to take it? What's the upside potential?

...but don't study it to death...

You've probably heard the expression "analysis paralysis." Well, outreach projects can fall victim to this when there's the feeling that every tiny detail has to be worked out before any move is made. As this book was being researched, it came to light that a good project had died on the vine when the congregation was led through a lengthy process by a well meaning but too cautious consultant.

There's no question that careful planning is necessary, but it's also clear that nothing at all will happen without taking some risk (see the *Insights* section, pp. 124-125).

...and make a specific plan.

Once again, use the checklist on p. 146 to outline your plan. Supplement it with whatever detail you need — letters of commitment from partners or funding sources, budgets, lists of volunteers, etc.

An important point: involve all sides in the planning. Be sure to include those you might work with and who would be your allies, such as social service agencies, and also those who would benefit from your outreach efforts, such as people who might live in the housing you would build or rehabilitate.

Community farmers in Livingston, California (story, p. 60), plan next steps for planting and harvesting with members of Our Redeemer Lutheran Church

Then...GO FOR IT!

Although you will have been "selling" your project all along, at the end you may have to sell it once more if you need the approval of the congregation or its leadership. If you're running into opposition, that's the time for leaders to reassert the needs, to point out the risks of not doing anything, and to clarify what risk is actually involved in going ahead. It's a time for the spark plugs and champions to reassert themselves against the naysayers. As the saying goes, "When the goin' gits tough, the tough git goin'!"

SUMMING UP
When You're Doing Outreach:

- Identify a real need.

- Don't be timid in your vision of the solution.

- Involve others in your vision, listen to them, enlist them as partners.

- Size up your resources, make a detailed and practical plan.

- Consider doing your project with another congregation or organization.

- Be flexible — modify your vision, your approach, if it seems necessary and reasonable.

- Don't just worry about money and other resources. Instead, spend your time and energy figuring out how you will get them.

- Tell your story compellingly, make your case.

- Don't underestimate people's willingness to pitch in once they understand the vision.

- Don't expect *everyone* to agree or join in your project — they may have "their own thing."

- Don't underestimate what your congregation can contribute—talents, skills, contacts, and material resources.

- Support other folks' outreach efforts if they seem valid — there's likely to be enough support for yours and theirs, too, especially since your "outreaching" congregation is likely to grow!

- Be willing to take risks . . . and *go for it*!

The following should be useful as you define the outreach direction you want to take. You can distribute the skills/interests questionnaire to members of your congregation to get the information needed to build a "people resources" inventory (see p. 143).

- **Outreach Brainstorming Options**
- **Members' Skills/Interests Questionnaire**
- **Needs We See**
- **Our Congregation's Own Needs**
- **Key Resources**
- **Our Preferences for Project Focus**
- **Potential Partners**
- **Project/Activity Selector**
- **Three Potential Projects**
- **Our Plan**
- **The Budget and Options for Obtaining Support**

Outreach Brainstorming Options
to define our direction

Possible Ways to Brainstorm

- ❐ Meeting

  Date/time/place _____

- ❐ Series of meetings

  Dates/times/place _____

- ❐ Retreat

  Date/time/ _____
  place/leader

- ❐ Other: _____

  _____

People to Invite

- ❐ Outreach people only
- ❐ Staff: _____
- ❐ Others: _____

  _____

  _____

- ❐ Congregation (all who would like to attend)
- ❐ Potential partners: _____

  _____

Skills / Interests / Connections
questionnaire for congregation members

Name _____ Today's date _____

Home address STREET _____

CITY/STATE/ZIP _____ Telephone No. _____

☐ Work full time   ☐ Retired/at home   ☐ Attend school full time days

☐ Work part time   ☐ Active volunteer   ☐ Attend school other times _____

☐ Raising children   ☐ Caring for relative   ☐ Other _____

Work for   NAME _____ Job/Occupation _____

LOCATION _____ Telephone No. _____

Attend school at NAME _____ Current grade _____ Field _____

Skills/Training *(for example, graphic design or computer training; 20 years as plumber; photography; etc.):*

_____

_____

Previous Jobs or Other Experience *(e.g., school volunteer; social work; house painting; etc.):*

_____

_____

Interests ☐ One-on-one service   ☐ Housing/neighborhoods

☐ Planning   ☐ Food/shelters

☐ Research   ☐ Jobs and Business Development

☐ Project Coordination   ☐ Health / Well-being

☐ Publicity   ☐ Education

☐ Volunteer coordination   ☐ Working with: ☐ kids ☐ adults ☐ seniors

☐ Fundraising   ☐ Projects: ☐ outside this community ☐ local

☐ Advocacy/political action   ☐ Other interests: _____

☐ Other: _____   _____

One or two projects/activities I'd especially like to do: _____

_____

Time available: ☐ Which weekdays: _____ ☐ Which nights: _____ ☐ Weekends: _____

Hours a week: ☐ 2   ☐ 5   ☐ 10   ☐ more _____

Willing to teach: ☐ Yes, I can teach others this skill: _____

Connections: ☐ Yes, ask me about people I know, other resources I can tap into for a project
(for example, a brother-in-law who is a plumber; surplus goods from work, etc.)

Comments: _____

_____

Key Resources
available or potentially available

OUR CONGREGATION

People
- ☐ Staff _____
  _____
- ☐ Project leaders _____
  _____
- ☐ Planning people _____
  _____
- ☐ Fundraisers _____
  _____
- ☐ Volunteer coordinators _____
  _____
- ☐ Others _____
  _____

Facilities and potential uses
- ☐ Sanctuary _____
  _____
- ☐ Classrooms _____
  _____
- ☐ Auditorium, large spaces
  _____
- ☐ Unused space / buildings
  _____
- ☐ Parking lot _____
  _____
- ☐ Land _____
  _____
- ☐ Other _____
  _____

Financial
- ☐ Outreach budget
  _____
- ☐ Outreach endowment
  _____
- ☐ Potential to raise $
- ☐ Other _____
  _____

OTHER ASSETS
- ☐ Volunteer time
- ☐ Members' skills
- ☐ Prestige / community contacts
- ☐ Our location _____
- ☐ Other _____
  _____

COMMUNITY

Businesses / Other Organizations
- ☐ Name: _____
  Contribution: _____
- ☐ Name: _____
  Contribution: _____
- ☐ Name: _____
  Contribution: _____

Volunteers
- ☐ Source: _____
  _____
- ☐ Source: _____
  _____
- ☐ Source: _____
  _____

Government
- ☐ Land/buildings: _____
- ☐ Funds: _____
- ☐ Staff or other: _____

OTHER

Local Denomination Office
- ☐ Funds
- ☐ Staff expertise
- ☐ Other _____

Foundations
- ☐ Name: _____
- ☐ Name: _____
- ☐ Name: _____

National Denomination
- ☐ Funds
- ☐ Staff expertise
- ☐ Other _____

State or Federal Government
- ☐ Program: _____
- ☐ Program: _____
- ☐ Program: _____

Ecumenical Organization
- ☐ Funds
- ☐ Staff expertise
- ☐ Other _____

Other
- ☐ Name: _____
- ☐ Name: _____
- ☐ Name: _____

Needs We See
in our community and beyond

Need	Location
_____	_____
_____	_____
_____	_____
_____	_____
_____	_____
_____	_____
_____	_____
_____	_____

Review those you have listed and: 1) check the three most pressing needs.
2) star the three our congregation might be best at addressing.

Our Own Congregation's Needs

Something for:
- ❏ people with lots of time
- ❏ people with limited time
- ❏ young people
- ❏ many people to do
- ❏ older people
- ❏ other: _____

Something that:
- ❏ revives congregational spirit
- ❏ deepens individual understanding
- ❏ crosses racial, ethnic lines
- ❏ crosses religious lines
- ❏ connects us to our community
- ❏ other: _____

Inreach Needs We Have
- ❏ job finding support
- ❏ other: _____

Other Needs We Have
- ❏ new members
- ❏ other: _____

Our Preferences for Project Focus

- ☐ Right near us
- ☐ Elsewhere in town
- ☐ Elsewhere in area
- ☐ Elsewhere in state
- ☐ Out of state
- ☐ Abroad

- ☐ Hands on
- ☐ Not hands on

- ☐ Inreach
- ☐ Outreach

- ☐ One-shot
- ☐ Continuing

- ☐ Service
- ☐ Education
- ☐ Social action
- ☐ Advocacy

- ☐ Alone
- ☐ With partner
- ☐ With several partners or group of congregations

- ☐ No cost/low cost
- ☐ Moderate cost
- ☐ Willing to raise substantial funds

- ☐ Something new
- ☐ Expand what we now do
- ☐ Revive or modify an old program

- ☐ Do It ourselves
- ☐ Start It and spin It off
- ☐ Set up as something separate

- ☐ Other _____

- ☐ Other _____

Potential Partners

Congregations

☐ Name: _____ ☐ Contact person: _____

☐ Name: _____ ☐ Contact person: _____

Other Possible Partners

☐ Name: _____ ☐ Contact person: _____

☐ Name: _____ ☐ Contact person: _____

Project / Activity Selector

Note: These are projects featured in the book; be sure to consider other possibilities as well.

Care and Access
- ❐ Caring for People at Home
- ❐ Meeting Emergency Needs
- ❐ Elder Day Care
- ❐ SHARE
- ❐ Eliminating Access Barriers
- ❐ Prisoners' Families
- ❐ Sponsoring Refugees
- ❐ Other: _____

Food and Shelters
- ❐ Cooking Food to Give, Sell
- ❐ Raising Food
- ❐ Soup Kitchens and Services
- ❐ Shelters/Services for Homeless
- ❐ Other: _____

Health and Well-Being
- ❐ Clinic Services
- ❐ Free Visits to the Doctor's Office
- ❐ A Mental Health Ministry
- ❐ Mobile Medical Care
- ❐ AIDS Ministries
- ❐ Other: _____

Jobs and Income
- ❐ Job-Finding Support
- ❐ Literacy Programs
- ❐ Summer Jobs for Youth
- ❐ Adult Job Training
- ❐ Creating a Bank
- ❐ Business Incubator
- ❐ Land To Farm
- ❐ Farmers Market
- ❐ Other: _____

Homes and Neighborhoods
- ❐ Building a Habitat House
- ❐ Fixing Up Houses
- ❐ Self-Help Construction
- ❐ Major Rehabilitation
- ❐ Homes on Your Property
- ❐ Transitional Housing, Services
- ❐ Making Financing Available
- ❐ Battling Drugs
- ❐ Neighborhood Renewal
- ❐ A Community Center
- ❐ Embracing Your Community
- ❐ Other: _____

Young People and Learning
- ❐ An After-School Program
- ❐ Pre-School
- ❐ Adopting a School
- ❐ Making College Possible
- ❐ Being a Mentor
- ❐ Focusing on Children
- ❐ Other: _____

Beyond Your Community
- ❐ Pairing With a Distant Congregation
- ❐ Making and Sending Things
- ❐ Sanctuary for the Oppressed
- ❐ Exporting Your Professional Expertise
- ❐ Young People Traveling to Serve
- ❐ Helping People Understand Poverty
- ❐ Other: _____

Other Ideas
- ❐ _____
- ❐ _____
- ❐ _____
- ❐ _____
- ❐ _____

Three Potential Projects

1 Description: _____
  Who, when, etc. _____

2 Description: _____
  Who, when, etc. _____

3 Description: _____
  Who, when, etc. _____

Our Plan

Goal / purpose: _____
_____

Description of project or activity: _____
_____
_____
_____

Phases, if any: 1) _____
2) _____
3) _____

Location/facilities to be used, cost if any: _____
_____

Duration of project or activity: _____
_____

Start-up Date: _____

Pilot test dates, if any: _____

Staff, if any (number, functions, cost): _____
_____

Volunteers (number, skills/interests): _____
_____

Guidance (*e.g., denominational staff or another congregation which has done it*): _____
_____

Partners, if any: _____
_____

Key People

Project Director: _____   Publicity: _____

Planning: _____   Fundraising: _____

Research: _____   People project will benefit: _____

Volunteer coordination: _____

_____   Other: _____

Overall cost: _____

Major source, amount of financial support: _____

Other resources (*e.g., donated goods or services*): _____

Evaluation dates: _____

The Budget
and options for obtaining support

Total Funds Needed
    Annually $ _____

    For start-up $ _____

Sources of Funds
- ❏ Congregation's budget $ _____
- ❏ Outreach budget $ _____
- ❏ Special offerings $ _____
- ❏ Special events $ _____
- ❏ Foundation support $ _____
- ❏ Business support $ _____

Fundraising methods
- ❏ Special offerings
- ❏ Individual appeals to members
- ❏ Tithe the congregation's budget
- ❏ Auction
- ❏ Fair
- ❏ Selling T-shirts, holding raffles, white elephant sales, etc.
- ❏ Other special fundraising events _____

    _____

- ❏ Seek foundation, business or other community support
- ❏ Other _____

    _____

Other sources of support
- ❏ Donation of goods and services _____
- ❏ Volunteers _____
- ❏ Volunteers from beyond the congregation _____
- ❏ Land or buildings from local government or others _____
- ❏ Partner's contributions _____

    _____

- ❏ Other _____

    _____

Detail your plan further if necessary

After you've made your commitment to a basic, sound plan, the more you can define just what steps you're going to take the better things are likely to go.

Recruit the right people

Most projects require a variety of skills: research, planning, project direction and coordination, volunteer recruitment and coordination, communications, and fundraising are among the most important. Some people may have several skills, but successful projects often have a small team of leaders, each with a different skill. Building that team can be critical for getting your project up and running successfully.

Board of Christian Mission Chair at Pawtucket Congregational Church in Rhode Island, checks her files.

Test your plan; make changes; persevere in the face of problems

Try to run a pilot before jumping in with both feet. You can then see how it goes and change your plan accordingly. Even without a pilot, as your program goes along you will want to keep flexible and change operational plans and strategies as you see the need.

You can count on problems arising. Some you can head off by planning for them from the start, but others you just won't be able to foresee. What you'll need then is both perseverance and resourceful problem solvers, to keep on track toward your goal.

At White Memorial Church in North Carolina, a group meets before evening counseling to review plans.

4. Think partners and neighbors

This is an attitude that should be uppermost in everyone's mind and heart: you are working in a partnership not only with your project partner, such as another congregation or a community development agency, but also with your people partners, your neighbors, the people whose lives your efforts focus on. All of you are working to solve problems together.

Working together on a learning center: All Souls Unitarian Church and Church of the Resurrection, New York City.

5. Continue to ask people's advice...

As you do your project, someone who's done it before can be invaluable for the fine points. If that person is nearby, so much the better. In any case, don't be reluctant to ask for help; most people love to share their expertise, especially in the kinds of projects you will be doing.

Volunteers from Congregational Church of Weston (left) and St. Gerard's Catholic Church confer on SHARE program details.

6. ...and use their materials as models

Why reinvent the wheel? An effective fundraising or program brochure can be very time consuming to create. Ask people if they will give you copies of their materials to use as models; be sure to ask how well they worked and what modifications they would suggest. In return, share the ones you prepare.

7 Be imaginative and resourceful in your fundraising

For almost any project or program, money is needed — sometimes a lot of it. The keys to successful fundraising are to be imaginative, both wide ranging and focused, forthright in stating your needs, and persistent.

Above all, make sure you do ask; don't assume that people will not respond — quite the contrary, they may give more than you expected, if you have made your case well. Present the facts and figures, as well as your vision and enthusiasm. And get the right person to do the asking — often the influence factor is crucial.

An important point: Outreach efforts can create "in" groups of people who are actually working on the projects. Your fundraising can make the rest of your congregation — and contributors beyond it, as well — feel like solid participants. Be sure to thank them, personally if possible, and let them know their contributions are key to making things happen. You may even want to consider giving contributors something, such as a certificate or a pin. Be sure to invite everyone to important milestones, such as a ground breaking.

Members of Church of the Pilgrims in Washington, D.C., helped re-build their organ to keep the project's costs down and make sure equal amounts were available for outreach.

In Fairfield, Connecticut, a joint choir concert nets $20,000 or more each year for the town's homeless shelter.

8 ▷ Volunteers: perhaps THE key to your success

In many, many programs, success really hinges on the effective recruitment, use and rewarding of volunteers. They need nurturing and supervision, structure and rewards. They need to be protected from burn-out. They need to be properly matched with jobs in terms of their own skills and interests, and they need to understand how their little piece fits into the whole and how they are making the project possible. Remember, your volunteers include not only the people who serve on the line in a soup kitchen, but also the people who do planning and fundraising.

Volunteer Scout leader (in rear) from All Souls Unitarian Church in New York City.

It's an enormously important subject and a vast one; we've touched on just one aspect on the next page, "Have some fun". Someone in your program should wear the hat of volunteer coordinator and really know their stuff; if you have a substantial number of volunteers, this should be the only hat they wear.

A must: If you will be depending on volunteers, make sure you have all the volunteers you will need — and some back-ups — before you start up. An after-school program, for instance, will fall flat on its face, and there will be a lot of disappointed youngsters, if the needed volunteers aren't there.

Bethany Presbyterian Church's literacy program tutors in Dayton, Ohio.

9 Have some fun: create a team and a team spirit

There are a lot of smiling faces in this book. Things always go better when people are having fun. Their energy level is up, they can get over rough spots more easily, they are more likely to be resourceful.

And having fun and getting to know others in the congregation may be major reasons some of your folks join an outreach effort — and stay with it! They're hungry for the friendships that often form, and they want to be part of a team that's doing something but also is enjoying it.

Union Station soup kitchen volunteers in Pasadena, California.

First Friends Meeting in Greensboro, North Carolina, used T-shirts as a spirit builder for their Habitat house team.

Finally, if you're clearly having fun, it's likely to spur more outreach efforts. It's also likely to make your congregation grow stronger as a community, as more of your people get to know each other better.

Tips: Celebrate even small victories. Get folks together just for fun. Tell some jokes, keep your meetings light. Reward people — even with something trivial — for a job or task well done. Mention them in your congregation's newsletter and at worship services during your progress reports. Design your projects so there are lots of opportunities to do things in pairs or as a group. Consider "badges" of some sort — T-shirts, for example. *Caution:* be sensitive to the possibility that others may feel they are "out" group.

10

Tutoring
Church helping kids with studies

Church builds Habitat project of its own

■ St. James Episcopal plans to build houses for the working poor.

Bayport church pursues AIDS ministry

Project a "journey in faith"

Peter and Barbara Thornton from Central Congregational in Providence, Rhode Island, with their newsletter on housing outreach efforts being undertaken by the church.

Beat the drum, trumpet the results!

It may sound like "strike up the band," but making noise — good noise — is very important. Let people know about your activities, particularly your successes. If your efforts help six people find jobs, let the congregation know it. If there were 150 people at the picnic for the school you've adopted, sound off!

In a world of frightening headlines and police blotter coverage on TV, people in your congregation are thirsting to know that good things are happening. If it's their own congregation that's creating the good news, so much the better.

A "moment for mission" is used by many congregations to herald the success of outreach activities. It's also a good way to announce volunteer opportunities and to give advance notice of a fundraiser. Very important, it's a chance to recognize individual achievements of outreach workers, and keep the congregation feeling part of the whole effort. If you have more than one outreach effort, speak about only one project during a particular moment for mission.

You may also want to have a printed hand-out, and be sure to put items in your newsletters. Finally, don't forget to supply the local newspapers, radio, TV and wire services with your news and pictures (or invite them to send reporters and photographers). The media are also eager to have good things to report.

Press coverage has two other important effects: it inspires other congregations to do outreach (fully a third of the congregations in this book came to our attention through news clips); and it can attract new members, people in your community who want to be part of a church or synagogue that is making a difference.

Outreach Beyond Outreach

**Making outreach happen
beyond your congregation**

*"Our opportunities to do good
are our talents."*

Cotton Mather

Outreach Beyond Outreach

Something most encouraging but quite unexpected came to light while talking about their Habitat for Humanity house project with the outreach people at First Friends in Greensboro, North Carolina. A woman on the Habitat team reported that she and some other employees in the company she works for had built a Habitat house, following the church's lead!

How wonderful to hear this kind of an outreach "echo" — a project that people had taken beyond their congregations and had duplicated in their work places or elsewhere in their lives.

What if we all did that? And not just with the particular outreach projects and programs we've done with our congregations, but by making altogether different contributions — where we work, in our neighborhoods, wherever we see the need and the possibility. On the next two pages are some activities featured in this book, plus a few more ideas; you can easily add to this list out of your own heart and imagination.

Then there's the possibility of getting other congregations in your area fired up, so that we usher in an "era of outreach." Included in this section are just a few ideas on that subject; hopefully they will trigger still more.

The woman second from the right is a member of First Friends Meeting in Greensboro, North Carolina. Some employees where she worked decided to build a Habitat house after hearing about her church's success and enjoyment building one. Pictured here are the steering committee and some members of the Habitat family.

Whether or not your congregation has something going, you can "make a difference" from other places in your life:

- **where you work**
- **at home**
- **through another organization**
- **with friends, neighbors or family members**

You can easily add to the possibilities listed. A social service agency or your own church or synagogue can screen prospects for you, if you can't identify people with needs. Organizations in your community can tell you about volunteer opportunities.

The family who will move into a Habitat for Humanity house that was built as an outreach project by some employees at the company where the woman on the left works.

Building or rehabilitating a house. You can organize a project team of people from work or your neighborhood, friends and family. Check with your local housing agencies, or see Habitat for Humanity in the *Resources* section listings.

Job referral. Maybe you know of a job opening where you work, or can refer someone to a friend who does.

As an employer. There are many options. If your company or organization can provide paid release time — perhaps 5% would be a goal — to employees to serve their communities, you would not only benefit others but also find the employees tremendously appreciative. Providing job training to the unemployed or underemployed is another way to help. Even if you have a very small business, you could offer a boy or girl who otherwise wouldn't have a crack at it, an after-school job or a summer job that would give them both income and work experience.

Your spare room. What about offering that spare room free or at low cost to someone who can't afford "market rate" housing? It might be an older person or someone in financial difficulty.

A child for the summer. You might take a child or a group of children on summer trips, or sponsor such trips, or camp.

A mentor relationship. Establishing an ongoing, one-on-one relationship can make an enormous difference to a younger person (see One to One in the *Resources* section listings; also, Big Brother/Big Sister in your area).

Volunteering in after-school or other programs. There are numerous volunteer opportunities to match your interests.

Providing free services. If you have a valuable service to offer — medical, dental, electrical, painting, etc. — you could offer it free or at very low cost.

Bertha Linquist (left), a volunteer at Newman Congregational in East Providence, Rhode Island, on a home visit.

Donating goods. Your business or organization may have surplus goods or materials — for example, computers that are too slow for your needs but still perfectly good — or you may have things at home that would be valuable donations.

Political action. Being active in supporting causes and taking a stand on specific issues can make needed change happen.

Increasing your available surplus. We all have potential surpluses right in our own pockets, and there are all sorts of ways to change the way we live to make that money available for things we want to support financially. For example, using energy more efficiently at home could save you hundreds of dollars a year. Multiply that by tens of millions of people, and there's a new source of billions of dollars available for making a difference.

YOUR IDEAS:

_____

_____

_____

_____

An Area-Wide Effort

Many of the problems of our times call for efforts from throughout the community. Getting lots of congregations involved is the key. If you can help this to happen, you will have made an enormous contribution.

Your own community comes first.

You can start by getting together with outreach people from other congregations in your immediate area, just to get to know each other and talk about outreach needs and potentials. You might suggest that your local clergy association be the organizer, or perhaps a congregation particularly active in outreach can issue the invitation and start things off by telling about what they've been doing.

Then see about something area-wide.

While an informal, networking approach may work well, one way to get going on an area-wide basis is to form an outreach association. This would be for all people in your area interested in outreach. Or you might ask an existing organization in your area to set up an outreach sub-group, rather than form a new organization. In either case the group's identity and focus on outreach should be clear.

There might be periodic get-togethers, a roster of all the churches, synagogues, organizations and their outreach people, and perhaps a directory of past and present projects.

One of the best kick-offs to a really vital area-wide effort might be an "outreach day." This could be in the form of a morning workshop with exhibits, followed by a bus tour to a few projects or program sites. There's no substitute for direct experience and contact, being there and talking with folks. Visiting a soup kitchen or a housing construction project or literacy program, for instance, will provide insights that people can't get otherwise — about how to run such a program, and about the people who need the service.

For any area-wide organization or events, be sure to include the following on your invitation lists: people from area and state conferences, denominational offices, ecumenical organizations, social service and development agencies and anyone else you can think of who might be interested in furthering a community-wide, congregation-focused effort. An interfaith call from an ecumenical organization may be the most appropriate way to invite people.

Find out what's happening; create resource materials.

Take a look at what's already happening: you may be surprised at how much is going on — churches and synagogues involved in all kinds of outreach efforts. It can be both a gold mine of experience and an aid in avoiding duplicating efforts.

Your denomination, clergy or ecumenical association may already know what's being done and have printed materials and videos. If not, suggest that they prepare them. Or, you and people from other congregations can pool information, compiling your own inventory. Someone — perhaps you, the reader — can make a video to share with folks in congregations throughout your area.

Figure out a way to coordinate things.

At some point, projects and programs that need doing should get sorted out. An area-wide outreach staff position might be created to help coordinate efforts. It could be jointly funded by the various denominations and ecumenical organizations, or one of the larger congregations might donate a staff person.

Toward an "era of outreach."

Just these efforts could move things strongly in the direction of an era of outreach in your area, but you're sure to think of still more things that can make it happen. Best of luck!

A GUIDE TO
HANDS-ON MISSION
IN MASSACHUSETTS

1990 Edition

Commission
on
Mission Development
and
Social Responsibility,

Massachusetts Conference
United Church of Christ

YOUR IDEAS:

_____

_____

_____

_____

Resources You Can Use

**Where to find helpful
people and information**

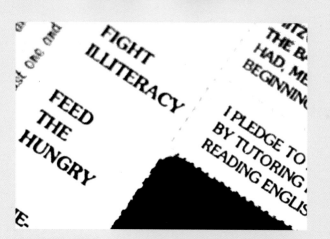

Ask and it shall be given unto you;
Seek and ye shall find;
Knock and it shall be opened unto you.

Matthew 7:7

Resources You Can Use

Volunteers serving sandwiches at Fort Street Presbyterian's soup kitchen.

I t may seem strange to you to start this with an interview with a volunteer (not shown here), but there's a good reason.

"I remember the first time I served dinner in a soup kitchen. There I was, up front, on the other side of the table, smiling and saying 'Hello, how are you' to a mix of disheveled people, some clearly in their cups, dishing out a hearty one dish meal to people who rapidly shuffled through the line, who said 'Thank you' at least twice or three times, ate rapidly, and then disappeared out the door as fast as possible.

"I didn't like it. You know? It put me in an awkward position of giving a handout. There didn't seem to be anything I could do to alter the experience for these folks . . . or to change their basic situation. And the gap between my healthy and stable life and their precarious ones . . . well, wow! And yet I realized that the meal I was serving was valuable to them. And there was a real kinship, you know, that I could feel with these homeless people, just because I was face to face with them, talking to them and 'reaching out' to help meet at least one of their basic needs."

The reason to include this story is to emphasize, for the umpteenth time, that there is no substitute for direct experience. So, whatever other resources you find listed in this section, don't forget to get yourself as much first-hand exposure and involvement as you can with the people and the possible settings in which you might do outreach!

THREE KEY POINTS

Don't limit your search

There are many wonderful sources of assistance and information available to you. Some of them will be right under your nose, quickly and easily accessed. But you may get rich rewards by going beyond your own area, becoming a real sleuth, and tapping many sources, even those pretty far afield. For example, a group from Summit Chapel, in Pennsylvania, traveled all the way to Missouri to learn how to make a MUV tractor (p. 84).

Volunteer coordinator in Pasadena AIDS center could tell much about what it takes to do it successfully.

Make a call, make a visit

Of special importance is talking directly with people, regardless of what you're looking for.   There's a wealth of information available to you by phone for just a few dollars and a small amount of time. So don't hesitate to telephone people; a half-hour phone conversation with someone who really knows the answers can be invaluable.

Even better is a visit, to see for yourself and possibly to try actually doing it — being on watch overnight in a shelter, working on a housing rehabilitation project, serving in a soup kitchen the way the man in the interview on the previous page did.

Be optimistic about your chances of success

The contacts you make who already have been down the road that you are considering are likely to be delighted to share with you. And if you're enthusiastic and have well worked out plans, the people that you ask to be volunteers or partners, or to fund your dream, will at least give you a hearing — and may well give you a resounding "Yes!" Remember, "Seek and ye shall find; knock and it shall be opened unto you."

Community loan fund development director explains how the fund works at the beginning of a tour for suburban congregation members.

SOURCES TO TAP

People you know can be especially helpful, particularly clergy and lay people in your own congregation who have ever been directly involved in outreach. They may have been part of a project before in another congregation, or have knowledge about a particular subject because of their training or work experience. They may also be able to suggest someone who has. Of course many are potential volunteers for involvement in the project, as well as sources of financial and 'in-kind' support.

Friends, relatives and colleagues at work or in other organizations to which you belong may also be excellent resources. And don't forget your old church or synagogue, which may be doing some exciting things.

Other congregations in your area should also be at the top of your list. With a few phone calls, you may be able to pinpoint another church or synagogue with the same activity you are considering. Their outreach people or clergy can tell you the pluses and minuses and show you the ropes. They may even have prepared printed or visual materials which would be helpful. They may also offer you the opportunity to join in their project, or possibly they will be a potential partner for you in a new project that would best be done jointly.

Your local clergy council is an ideal place to look for prior experience, ideas for resources and potential partners. Brainstorming and brainpicking at a joint meeting of local outreach committees can also produce results for you.

Ecumenical organizations in your metropolitan area or your state frequently have people who specialize in outreach or who know what's being done and by whom. Some have special areas of interest and programs to match. They may be able to help you put together an ecumenical or interfaith project. In this section is a nationwide list of selected ecumenical and interfaith councils. Additional listings may be found in the *Yearbook of American and Canadian Churches*.

Your denomination is among the first places to contact. National and regional offices usually have helpful and knowledgeable staff specializing in outreach. Many of the congregations whose stories are featured in this book were brought to light by denominational staff.

Denominations also frequently have outreach programs of their own in which individual congregations can participate — overseas mission programs, summer work camps for youth, etc. They also offer publications and often videos, and there may well be some outreach titles of value in your efforts. Most also publish a denominational directory listing all the local congregations, with clergy names and telephone numbers, a helpful aid in making your contacts. There may also be denominational monies to help fund your efforts; be sure to ask about these.

The Handbook of Denominations in the United States lists over 225 religious bodies. Listings of many headquarters and of regional and local offices may be found in the *Yearbook of American and Canadian Churches*.

Books on outreach and guides for carrying out specific programs can provide you with additional "how to" insights. Some of the better ones are listed on p. 187. Additional copies of this book can be used to illustrate the reality of what you're considering and to increase enthusiasm in your own congregation; you'll find ordering information inside the back cover. There may also be a video available before long.

Keep your eyes and ears open for church and synagogue programs that may be featured in the **media**. About a quarter of the congregations written up in this book came to our notice through news clips and even a radio program. Denominational and other **religious periodicals** can be an excellent source as well. Frequently there's a good deal of detail and names of people who can fill you in if you just give them a call.

Communications and fundraising aids can be a big help. You may find that another congregation has developed just what you

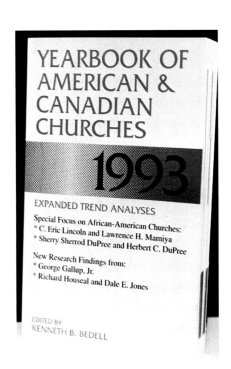

YEARBOOK OF AMERICAN & CANADIAN CHURCHES 1993

EXPANDED TREND ANALYSES

Special Focus on African-American Churches:
* C. Eric Lincoln and Lawrence H. Mamiya
* Sherry Sherrod DuPree and Herbert C. DuPree

New Research Findings from:
* George Gallup, Jr.
* Richard Houseal and Dale E. Jones

EDITED BY
KENNETH B. BEDELL

need — a brochure, for instance, or the Tikun Olam card (see p. 96). To avoid reinventing the wheel, you may be able to use something "as is" or modify it a bit. Be sure to ask about these materials when you talk with another congregation about their program. There are also some products available through denominational catalogs or from commercial sources.

Foundations are potential financial partners for you, and indeed they may be critical to the success of your efforts. If you have a friend who's familiar with fundraising, he or she may be able to help you identify potential funding sources. In addition to the larger foundations, don't neglect to look into small family foundations (lawyers handling family affairs often know of some).

Local companies may also be sympathetic to your objectives and can be a rich source of volunteers, supplies, or in-kind contributions, as well as funding.

Independent nationwide programs will also be good resources for you. There are a great many of these. The four included in the following resource listings were chosen because of the importance of their central concepts, the change in mind-set they engender, and the technical assistance they provide to congregations wanting to start programs. They are also excellent programs for Outreach Beyond Outreach (see p. 159).

Habitat for Humanity (story p. 65)

One to One (story p. 49)

Community Development Loan Funds (story p. 73)

SHARE (story p. 19)

RESOURCE LISTINGS

Selected State and Regional Ecumenical Organizations

(Additional listings may be found in the *Yearbook of American and Canadian Churches*)

Alabama

Greater Birmingham Ministries, 1205 North 25th Street, Birmingham AL 35234-3197, (205) 326-6821

Interfaith Mission Service, 411-B Holmes Ave., Huntsville AL 35801, (205) 536-2401

Alaska

Alaska Christian Conference, Rev. Jean Straatmeyer, 1375 W. Bogard Rd., Wasilla AL 99654

Interfaith Council of Anchorage, Rev. Rick Cavens, St. Mark Lutheran Church, 3230 Lake Otis Pkwy., Anchorage AL 99504, (907) 276-6231

Arizona

Arizona Ecumenical Council, 4423 N. 24th St., Ste. 750, Phoenix AZ 85016, (602) 468-3818

Arkansas

Arkansas Interfaith Conference, 16th & Louisiana, PO Box 151, Scott AR 72142, (501) 961-2626

California

Northern California Ecumenical Council, 942 Market Street, 3rd, San Francisco CA 94102, (415) 434-0670

Southern California Ecumenical Council, 1010 S. Flower,ste. 403, Los Angeles CA 90015, (213) 746-7677

Colorado

Colorado Council of Churches, 1234 Bannock St., Denver CO 80204, (303) 825-4910

Interfaith Council of Boulder, 2650 Table Mesa Dr., Boulder CO 80303, (303) 499-1444

Connecticut

Christian Conference of Connecticut (CHRISCON), 60 Lorraine St., Hartford CT 06105, (203) 236-4281

Council of Churches and Synagogues of Lower Fairfield County, 628 Main St., Stamford CT 06901, (203) 348-2800

District of Columbia

The Council of Churches of Greater Washington, 411 Rittenhouse St., NW, Washington DC 20011, (202) 722-9240

Delaware

The Christian Council of Delaware and Maryland's Eastern Shore, 1626 N. Union St., Wilmington DE 19806, (302) 655-6151

Florida

Christian Service Center for Central Florida, Inc., 808 West Central Blvd., Orlando FL 32805-1809, (407) 425-2523

Florida Council of Churches, 924 N. Magnolia Ave., Ste. 236, Orlando FL 32803, (407) 839-3454

Georgia

Christian Council of Metropolitan Atlanta, 465 Boulevard, SE, Atlanta GA 30312, (404) 622-2235

Georgia Christian Council, PO Box 7193, Macon GA 31209, (912) 743-2085

Hawaii

Hawaii Council of Churches, 1300 Kailua Rd., B-1, Kailua HI 96734, (808) 263-9788

Idaho

The Regional Council for Christian Ministry, Inc., PO Box 2236, Idaho Falls ID 83403, (208) 524-9935

Illinois

Evanston Ecumenical Action Council, PO Box 1414, Evanston IL 60204, (708) 475-1150

Illinois Conference of Churches, 615 S. 5th St., Springfield IL 62703, (217) 544-3423

Oak Park-River Forest Community of Congregations, 324 N. Oak Park Ave., Oak Park IL 60302

Indiana

The Church Federation of Greater Indianapolis, Inc., 1100 W. 42nd St., Ste. 345, Indianapolis IN 46208, (317) 926-5371

Indiana Council of Churches, 1100 W. 42nd St., Rm. 225, Indianapolis IN 46208-3383, (317) 923-3674

Interfaith Community Council, Inc., 702 E. Market St., New Albany IN 47150, (812) 948-9248

Iowa

Churches United, Inc., 866 - 4th Ave. SE, Cedar Rapids IA 52403, (319) 366-7163

Ecumenical Ministries of Iowa (EMI), 3816 - 36th St., Ste. 202, Des Moines IA 50310, (515) 255-5905

Kansas

Cross-Lines Cooperative Council, 1620 S. 37th St., Kansas City KS 66106, (913) 281-3388

Kansas Ecumenical Ministries, 5942 SW 29th St., Topeka KS 66614, (913) 272-9531

Kentucky

Association of Community Ministries, 1115 S. 4th St., Louisville KY 40203, (502) 589-7710

Kentuckiana Interfaith Community, 1115 South 4th St., Louisville KY 40203-3101, (502) 587-6265

Kentucky Council of Churches, 1039 Goodwin Dr., Lexington KY 40505, (606) 253-3027

Louisiana

Louisiana Interchurch Conference, 660 N. Foster Dr., Ste. A-225, Baton Rouge LA 70806, (504) 924-0213

Greater Baton Rouge Federation of Churches & Synagogues, PO Box 626, Baton Rouge LA 70821, (504) 925-3414

Maine

Maine Council of Churches, 15 Pleasant Ave., Portland ME 04103, (207) 772-1918

Maryland

Central Maryland Ecumenical Council, Cathedral House, 4E. University Pkwy., Baltimore MD 21218, (410) 467-6194

Community Ministry of Montgomery County, 114 W. Montgomery Ave., Rockville MD 20850, (301) 762-8682

Massachusetts

Cooperative Metropolitan Ministries, 474 Centre St., Newton MA 02158, (617) 244-3650

Massachusetts Council of Churches, 14 Beacon St., Boston MA 02108, (617) 523-2771

Worcester County Ecumenical Council, 25 Crescent St., Worcester, MA 01605, (508) 757-8385

Michigan

Christian Communication Council of Metro Detroit, 1300 Mutual Building, 28 W. Adams, Detroit MI 48226, (313) 962-0340

Greater Detroit Interfaith Roundtable, PO Box 2249, 150 W. Boston, Detroit MI 48202, (313) 869-6306

Michigan Ecumenical Forum, 809 Center St., Ste. 7-B, Lansing MI 48906, (517) 485-4395

Selected State and Regional Ecumenical Organizations (continued)

Minnesota
Greater Minneapolis Council of Churches, 122 W. Franklin Ave., Rm. 218, Minneapolis MN 55404, (612) 870-3660
Minnesota Council of Churches, 122 W. Franklin Ave., #100, Minneapolis MN 55404, (612) 870-3600
St. Paul Area Council of Churches, 1671 Summit Ave., St. Paul MN 55105, (612) 646-8805

Mississippi
Mississippi Religious Leadership Conference, PO Box 68123, Jackson MS 39286-8123, (601) 948-5954

Missouri
Council of Churches of the Ozarks, PO Box 3947, Springfield MO 65808-3947, (417) 862-3586
Ecumenical Ministries, #2 St. Louis Ave., Fulton MO 65251, (314) 642-6065

Montana
Montana Association of Churches, Andrew Square, Ste. G, 100 24th St. W., Billings MT 59102, (406) 656-9779

Nebraska
Interchurch Ministries of Nebraska, 215 Centennial Mall S., Rm. 411, Lincoln NE 68508-1888, (402) 476-3391
Lincoln Interfaith Council, 215 Centennial Mall S., Rm. 411, Lincoln NE 68508, (402) 474-3017

New Hampshire
New Hampshire Council of Churches, 24 Warren St., PO Box 1107, Concord NH 03302, (603) 224-1352

New Jersey
Metropolitan Ecumenical Ministry, 525 Orange St., Newark NJ 07107, (201) 481-6650
New Jersey Council of Churches, 116 N. Oraton Pkwy., East Orange NJ 07017, (201) 675-8600

New Mexico
Inter-Faith Council of Santa Fe, New Mexico, 818 Camino Sierra Vista, Santa Fe NM 87501, (505) 983-2892
New Mexico Conference of Churches, 124 Hermosa SE, Albuquerque NM 87108-2610, (505) 255-1509

New York
The Council of Churches of the City of New York, 475 Riverside Dr., Rm. 439, New York NY 10015, (212) 870-2120
New York State Council of Churches, Inc., 362 State St., Albany NY 12210, (518) 436-9319

North Carolina
Greensboro Urban Ministry, 407 N. Eugene St., Greensboro NC 27401, (919) 271-5959
North Carolina Council of Churches, Methodist Bldg.,1307 Glenwood Ave., 162, Raleigh NC 27605-3258, (919) 828-6501

North Dakota
North Dakota Conference of Churches, 227 W. Broadway, Bismarck ND 58501, (701) 255-0604
Ohio
Interchurch Council of Greater Cleveland, 2230 Euclid Ave., Cleveland OH 44115-2499, (216) 621-5925
Ohio Council of Churches, Inc., 89 E. Wilson Bridge Rd., Columbus OH 43085-2391, (614) 885-9590

Oklahoma
Oklahoma Conference of Churches, PO Box 60288, Oklahoma City OK 73146, (405) 525-2928
Tulsa Metropolitan Ministry, 221 S. Nogales, Tulsa OK 74127, (918) 582-3147

Oregon

Ecumenical Ministries of Oregon, 0245 SW Bancroft Street, Suite B, Portland OR 97201, (503) 221-1054

Pennsylvania

Northwest Interfaith Movement, 6757 Greene St., 3rd Floor, Philadelphia PA 19119, (215) 843-5600
The Pennsylvania Council of Churches, 900 S. Arlington Ave., Ste. 100, Harrisburg PA 17109, (717) 545-4761

Rhode Island

The Rhode Island State Council of Churches, 734 Hope St., Providence RI 02906, (401) 861-1700

South Carolina

South Carolina Christian Action Council, Inc., PO Box 3663, Columbia SC 29230, (803) 786-7115

South Dakota

Association of Christian Churches, 1320 S. Minnesota Ave., Ste. 210, Sioux Falls SD 57105, (605) 334-1980

Tennessee

Metropolitan Inter Faith Association (MIFA), PO Box 3130, Memphis TN 38173-0130, (901) 527-0208

Texas

Greater Dallas Community of Churches, 2800 Swiss Ave., Dallas TX 75204, (214) 824-8680
Interfaith Ministries for Greater Houston, 3217 Montrose Blvd., Houston TX 77006-3980, (713) 522-3955
Texas Conference of Churches, 6633 Hwy. 290 East, Ste. 200, Austin TX 78723-1157, (512) 451-0991

Utah

The Shared Ministry, 175 W. 200 S., Ste. 3006, Salt Lake City UT 84101, (801) 355-0168

Vermont

Vermont Ecumenical Council and Bible Society, 285 Maple St., Burlington VT 05401, (802) 864-7723

Virginia

Community Ministry of Fairfax County, 1920 Association Dr., Rm 505, Reston VA 22091, (703) 620-5014
Virginia Council of Churches, Inc., 1214 W. Graham Rd., Ste. 3, Richmond VA 23220-1409, (804) 321-3300

Washington

Associated Ministries of Tacoma-Pierce County, 1224 South "I" St., Tacoma WA 98405, (206) 383-3056
Church Council of Greater Seattle, 4759 - 15th Ave., NE, Seattle WA 98105, (206) 525-1213
Spokane Christian Coalition, E. 245 - 13th Ave., Spokane WA 99202, (509) 624-5156

West Virginia

The Greater Wheeling Council of Churches, 110 Methodist Bldg., Wheeling WV 26003, (304) 232-5315
West Virginia Council of Churches, 1608 Virginia St. E., Charleston WV 25311, (304) 344-3141

Wisconsin

Interfaith Conference of Greater Milwaukee, 1442 N. Farwell Ave., Ste. 200, Milwaukee WI 53202, (414) 276-9050
Wisconsin Conference of Churches, 1955 W. Broadway, Ste. 104, Madison WI 53713, (608) 222-9779

Wyoming

Wyoming Church Coalition, PO Box 990, Laramie WY 82070, (307) 745-6000

Habitat for Humanity (see pp. 6, 65)

There are nearly 1,000 local affiliates (i.e., local organizations) to help you and your congregation get a project under way. To find out about a local affiliate in your area or how to start one, call or write the regional office that covers your state, or the national Habitat office.

National Headquarters:
Habitat for Humanity International, Inc., 121 Habitat Street, Americus GA 31709-3498, (912) 924-6935 or 1-800-HABITAT

Regional Centers:

Northern US
Peter Beard, Director, 121 Habitat Street, Americus GA 31709, (912) 924-6935, ext. 134

Western US
Carol Gregory, Director, 121 Habitat Street, Americus GA 31709, (912) 924-6935, ext. 508

Northeast (CT, ME, MA, NH, NY, RI, VT)
Barbara Yates, Dir.; Brenda Mleziva, Assoc. Dir.; PO Box 2322, Acton MA 01720, (508) 486-4421

Mid-Atlantic (DE, NJ, PA)
Jean Shipman, PO Box 4984, Lancaster PA 17604-4984, (717)399-9592

Mideast (IN, OH)
Hubert and Fran Ping, PO Box 30, Lebanon IN 46052, (317) 482-4684

East (DC, MD, VA, WV)
Claire Martindale, PO Box 1403 , Harrisonburg VA 22801, (703) 564-5301

South Atlantic (NC, SC)
Sandra Graham, Dir.; Gib Edson, Assoc. Dir., PO Box 1712, Easley SC 29640, (803) 855-1102

South Central (TN, KY)
Sara Coppler, Assoc. Dir.; 248 East Short Street, Lexington KY 40507, (606) 233-7614

Midwest (IL, MI, WI)
Bill Ward, Dir.; Robert Hall, Assoc. Dir.; 1920 South Laflin, Chicago IL 60608, (312) 243-6448

Upper Midwest (IA, MN, ND, SD)
Mark Abraham, Dir.; PO Box 23316, Minneapolis MN 55423-0316, (612) 866-7873
Austin Keith, Assoc. Dir., American Indian Affairs, PO Box 1090, Eagle Butte SD 57625, (605) 964-8530

South (AL, LA, MS)
Jay Collins, PO Box 112, Tupelo MS 38802-0112, (601) 844-2397

Southeast (FL, GA)
Gene Crumley, Habitat for Humanity, 121 Habitat Street, Americus GA 31709, (912) 924-6935, Ext 530

Heartland (AR, KS, MO, NE)

Carolyn Talboys, PO Box 8955, Springfield MO 65801-8955, (417) 831-0982

Southwest (OK, TX)

Joe Gatlin, Dir.; Keith Branson, Assoc. Dir.; PO Box 3005, Waco TX 76707, (817) 756-7575

Regina Nobles, Development Dir., 5446 Richmond St, Dallas TX 75206, (214) 826-1742

Rocky Mountain (CO, NM, UT, WY)

Ray Finney, 1331 East 31st Ave., Denver CO 80205, (303) 296-0978

West (AZ, CA, HI, NV)

Ken Karlstad, Dir., 550 East Chapman Avenue, Orange CA 92666, Ste. C, (714) 744-8414

Julia Janecki, Assoc. Dir., 1924 Trinity Avenue, Walnut Creek CA 94596, (510) 937-0753

Northwest (AK, ID, MT, OR, WA)

Les Alford, Dir.; Annis Henson, Assoc. Dir.; 566 NE Clay Avenue, Bend OR 97701, (503) 383-4637

SHARE (see p. 19)

(see p. 19)

Regional centers can help you and your congregation get a project under way. If there is no office or local program listed for your area, be sure to call national headquarters to see if one has recently been opened.

National Headquarters:
World SHARE, Inc., 3350 E Street, San Diego CA 92102, (619) 525-2200

Regional Centers:

Arizona
FoodSHARE-Phoenix, 2841 N. 31st Avenue, #2, Phoenix AZ 85009, (602) 272-3663

Colorado
SHARE-Colorado, 9360 Federal Blvd., Federal Heights CO 80221, (303) 428-0400, (800) 933-7427

District of Columbia
SHARE-Washington, DC, 5170 Lawrence Place, Hyattsville MD 20781, (301) 864-3115

Florida
SHARE - Central Florida, 1969 W. New Hampshire Street, Orlando FL 32803, (407) 858-0300, (800) 726-7427
SHARE-Tampa Bay, 1405 E. 2nd Avenue, Tampa FL 33605, (813) 248-3379

Georgia
SHARE-Georgia, c/o Atlanta Food Bank, 970 Jefferson St., NW, Atlanta GA 30318, (404) 892-9822

Illinois
ComeSHARE (IL), 1222 Bunn Avenue, Springfield IL 62703, (217) 529-2500
SHARE of Central Illinois, 1825 NE Adams Street, Peoria IL 61603, (309) 637-0282
SHARE-Rockford, 320 S. Avon, Rockford IL 61102, (815) 961-7328

Iowa
SHARE-Iowa, PO Box 328, Oskaloosa IA 52577-0328, (515) 673-4000

Kansas
Heartland SHARE, 215 SE Quincy, Topeka KS 66603, (913) 234-6208

Maryland
SHARE-Baltimore, 808 Barkwood Ct., Linthicum MD 21090, (410) 636-9615

Michigan
SHARE-Mid Michigan, 1735 Blair Street, Lansing MI 48910, (517) 482-8900

Minnesota
Fare SHARE (MN), 807 Hampden Avenue, St. Paul MN 55114, (612) 644-6003

New England
SHARE-New England, PO Box 63, Canton MA 02021, (617) 828-5151, (800) 874-2730

New Jersey
SHARE-New Jersey, PO Box 5427, Newark NJ 07105-3909, (201) 344-2400

New York
SHARE-New York, 1601 Bronxdale Avenue, Bronx NY 10462, (718) 518-1513

North Carolina
SHARE-Heart of the Carolinas, PO Box 2009, Fayetteville NC 28302, (919) 485-6923

Ohio
SHARE-Northern Ohio, PO Box 2000, Akron OH 44309, (216) 376-7730

Pennsylvania
SHARE-Philadelphia, 2901 W. Hunting Park Avenue, Philadelphia PA 19129, (215) 223-2220

Tri-State (western PA, eastern OH, northern WV)
Tri-State SHARE, 415 11th Street, Ambridge PA 15003, (412) 266-0470

Virginia
SHARE-Hampton Roads, 1115 Tabb Avenue, Norfolk VA 23504, (804) 627-6599
SHARE-Virginia, PO Box 570, Christiansburg VA 24073, (703) 381-1185

Wisconsin
SHARE of SE Wisconsin, 13111 W. Silver Spring Drive, Butler WI 53007

Community Development Loan Funds (see p. 73)

The following are members of the National Association of Community Development Loan Funds. If there is no fund listed for your area, be sure to call the National Association office to see if one has recently been established. (**H**)=housing development, (**B**)=business development

National
National Association of Community Development Loan Funds, 924 Cherry Street, Philadelphia, PA 19107, 215-923-4754

Funds, by State:
Arizona
MICRO, 802 E. 46th St., Tucson AZ 85713, (602) 622-3553 (B)

California
Northern California Community Loan Fund, 14 Precita Ave., San Francisco CA 94110, (415) 431-1488 (H/B)
Rural Community Assistance Corporation, 2125 19th St., Ste. 203, Sacramento CA 95818, (916) 447-2854 (H)
Low Income Housing Fund, 605 Market St., Ste. 200, San Francisco CA 94105, (415) 777-9804 (H/B)

Connecticut
Cooperative Fund of New England, 108 Kenyon St., Hartford CT 06105, (203) 523-4305 (H/B)
Greater New Haven Community Loan Fund, 5 Elm St., New Haven CT 06510, (203) 789-8690 (H)

District of Columbia
Washington Area Community Investment Fund, 2201 P St., NW, Washington DC 20037, (202) 462-4727 (H)

Georgia
Southeastern Reinvestment Ventures, 159 Ralph McGill Blvd., NE, Rm 506, Atlanta GA 30308, (404) 659-0002 x 3240 (H/B)

Illinois
Chicago Community Loan Fund, 343 South Dearborn, Ste. 1001, Chicago IL 60604, (312) 922-1350 (H/B)
Illinois Facilities Fund, 300 W. Adams St., Ste. 431, Chicago IL 60606-5101, (312) 629-0060 (B)

Iowa
Anawim Fund of the Midwest, 517 W. 7th, PO Box 4022, Davenport IA 52808, (319) 324-6632 (B/H)

Kentucky
Federation of Appalachian Housing Enterprises, Drawer B, Berea KY 40403, (606) 986-2321 (H)
HEAD Corp. Revolving Loan Fund, PO Box 504, Berea KY 40403, (606) 986-3283 (B)

Maryland
McAuley Institute, 8300 Colesville Rd., Ste. 310, Silver Spring MD 20910, (301) 588-8110 (H)

Massachusetts
Boston Community Loan Fund, 30 Germania St., Jamaica Plain MA 02130, (617) 522-6768 (H)
Industrial Cooperative Association RLF, 20 Park Plaza, Ste. 1127, Boston MA 02116, (617)338-0010 (B)
Institute for Community Economics RLF, 57 School St., Springfield MA 01105-1331, (413) 746-8660 (H/B)
Worcester Community Loan Fund, PO Box 271, Mid-Town Mall, Worcester MA 01614, (508) 799-6106 (H/B)

Michigan
Michigan Housing Trust Fund, 3401 E. Saginaw, Ste. 212, Lansing MI 48912, (517) 336-9919 (H)

Minnesota
Northcountry Cooperative Development Fund, 400 19th Ave. So., Ste. 202, Minneapolis MN 55454, (612) 339-1553 (H/B)

Nebraska
McAuley Housing Fund, 1650 Farnum St., Omaha NE 68102, (402) 346-6000 x344 (H)

New Hampshire
New Hampshire Community Loan Fund, Box 800, 79 South State St., Concord NH 03302, (603) 224-6669 (H/B)

New Mexico
New Mexico Community Development Loan Fund, PO Box 705, Albuquerque NM 87103, (505) 243-3196 (H/B)

New Jersey
New Jersey Community Loan Fund, PO Box 1655, Trenton NJ 08607, (609) 989-7766 (H/B)

New York
Capital District Community Loan Fund, 340 First St., Albany NY 12206, (518) 436-8586 (H/B)
Leviticus 25:23 Alternative Fund, 299 North Highland Ave., Ossining NY 10562, (914) 941-9422 (H/B)
Nonprofit Facilities Fund, 12 West 31st St., New York NY 10001, (212) 868-6710 (B)

North Carolina
Self-Help Ventures Fund, 413 East Chapel Hill St., Durham NC 27701, (919) 683-3016 (H/B)

Ohio
Common Wealth Revolving Loan Fund, 1221 Elm St., Youngstown OH 44505, (216) 744-2667 (H/B)
Cornerstone-Homesource Regional Loan Fund, PO Box 6842, Cincinnati OH 45206, (513) 651-1505 (H)

Oklahoma
Forge, Inc., Rt. 6, Box 134-1, Tahlequah OK 74464, (501) 443-7205 (B)

Oregon
ARABLE, 715 Lincoln St., Eugene OR 97401, (503) 485-7630 (B)

Pennsylvania
Community Loan Fund of SW PA, 48 South 14th St., Pittsburgh PA 15203, (412) 381-9965 (H/B)
Delaware Valley Community Reinvestment Fund, 924 Cherry St., 3rd Fl., Philadelphia PA 19107, (215) 925-1130 (H/B)
Fund for an OPEN Society, 311 S. Juniper St., Ste. 400, Philadelphia PA 19107, (215) 735-6915 (H)

South Dakota
Lakota Fund, PO Box 340, Kyle SD 57752, (605) 455-2500 (B)

Texas
Berakah Alternative Investment Fund, 925 S. Mason, Ste. 131, Katy TX 77450, (713) 392-3838 (H/B)

Vermont
Vermont Community Loan Fund, PO Box 827, Montpelier VT 05601, (802) 223-1448 (H/B)

Washington
Cascadia Revolving Fund, 157 Yesler Way, Ste. 414, Seattle WA 98104, (206) 447-9226 (H/B)

One to One (see p.49)

(see p.49)

If your area is not listed here, call or write the One to One National Headquarters to see if they have started or plan a program near you.

National
One to One Partnership, Inc., 2801 M Street, NW, Washington DC 20007, (202) 338-3844

California: Los Angeles, Sacramento areas
California One to One, Patrice A. Théard, Exec. Dir., 333 South Grand Ave, Suite 1800, Los Angeles CA 90071, (213) 617-5802

District of Columbia
One to One Partnership, Inc., Siddhi Shonibaré, Reg'l Mngr., 2801 M Street, NW, Washington DC 20007, (202) 338-3844
One to One Partnership, Inc., Harold L. Brinkley, Vice Pres., 2801 M Street, NW, Washington DC 20007, (202) 338-3844

Georgia: Atlanta area
One to One Atlanta, Trojanell B. Wilson, Exec. Dir., 127 Peachtree Street, NE, Suite 702, Atlanta GA 30303, (404) 681-3755

Massachusetts: Greater Boston area
Greater Boston One to One, Linda Alioto-Robinson, Exec. Dir., Two Liberty Sq., 9th Floor, Boston MA 02109, (617) 422-6770

Michigan: Detroit area
One to One Detroit, Crescenda A. Mickels, Exec. Dir., 12255 Camden Street, Detroit MI 48213, (313) 352-3110

Nebraska: Omaha area
One to One Omaha, Michael D. Hanson, Dir., United Way of the Midlands, 1805 Harney Street, Omaha NE 68102, (402) 342-8232, ext. 532

New Jersey: Newark area
One to One New Jersey, William D. Payne, Exec. Dir., 33 Washington Street, 2nd Floor, Newark NJ 07102, (201) 242-1142

New York: New York City, Long Island (two offices)
One to One New York, Robin A. Smith, Exec. Dir., 375 Park Ave., Ste. 301, New York, NY 10152, (212) 339-0141
One to One Long Island, Joan S. Brennan, Exec. Dir., 90 Merrick Ave., East Meadow, NY 11554, (516) 228-9000

Pennsylvania: Philadelphia area
One to One Philadelphia, Mary W. Strasser, Exec. Dir., 7 Benjamin Franklin Pkwy, 3rd, Philadelphia PA 19103, (215) 665-2467

Virginia: Richmond area
One to One Richmond, James T. Starnes, Exec. Dir., 805 East Broad Street, 10th Floor, Richmond VA 23219, (804) 786-8732

Index of Congregations in this book

The capacities of these churches and synagogues to respond to requests for more information will vary. Please be understanding of any limitations.

Index of Congregations in this Book (continued)

Metropolitan Baptist Church, 808 North A Street, Pensacola, FL, 32501; (904) 434-2678; Reverend Dave Thomas; 400 parishioners; urban; p. 52.

Mt. Nebo AME Church, (African Methodist Episcopal); PO Box 656, College Station, Little Rock, AR, 72053; (501) 490-0561; Reverend H. D. Stewart; 900 congregants; urban; p. 75.

Newman Congregational Church, (United Church of Christ); PO Box 4764, Rumford, RI, 02916; (401) 434-4742; Reverend David F. Shire; 600 members; suburban; p. 20.

Old Cambridge Baptist Church, 1151 Massachusetts Ave., Cambridge, MA, 02138; (617) 864-8068; Reverend Irv Cummings; urban; p. 90.

Oreland Presbyterian Church, 1119 Church Road, Oreland PA 19075; (215) 887-7002; Stephen Shirk, Youth Minister; 849 members; suburban; p. 87.

Our Lady of the Woods, (Roman Catholic); PO Box 416, Woodland Park, CO, 80866; (719) 687-9159; Father Karl Useldinger; Coordinator Greg Shilling: 719-548-2258; 250 households; rural; p. 22.

Our Redeemer Lutheran Church, 1505 E Street, Livingston, CA, 95334; (209) 394-7613, Reverend Bill Ruth; 85 members; rural; p. 60.

Pawtucket Congregational Church, (United Church of Christ); 40 Walcott Street, Pawtucket, RI, 02860; (401) 722-7934; Reverend Dr. George E. Peters; 290 members; urban; p. 71.

Ridge Evangelical Lutheran Church, 2501 West 103rd Street, Chicago, IL, 60655; (312) 445-6922; Reverend Cynthia Hileman; 640 members; urban; p. 22.

Santa Fe Episcopal Church, 1108 Brunswick, San Antonio, TX, 78211;(210) 923-0822; The Reverend Will Waters; 75 families; urban; p. 78.

Sayville Congregational Church, (United Church of Christ); 131 Middle Road, Sayville, NY, 11782; (516) 589-1519; The Reverend John A. Geter Jr.; 500 members; town; p. 134.

Scott Memorial United Methodist Church, 10372 West Chicago Blvd, Detroit, MI, 48204; (313) 931-6280; Dr. Andrew Allie, Pastor; 400 adult members; inner city; p. 48.

Second Baptist Church, 222 East 8th and Cumberland, Little Rock, AR, 72202; (501) 374-9284; Reverend Billy White; 800 members; urban; p. 75.

Second Grace United Methodist Church, 18700 Joy Road, Detroit, MI, 48228; (313) 838-6475; Reverend Emmanuel Bailey; 200 members; inner city; p. 47.

Seventh Day Adventist Church, Barbertown, OH, 44203; (216) 745-6800; Greg Schaller, Pastor; Barberton Community Service Center, 223 2nd St NW, 216-848-3225; 130 members; town; p. 25.

Southminster Presbyterian Church, 7001 Far Hills Ave., Dayton, OH, 45459; (513) 433-1810; Reverend Robert Smith; 550 households; suburban; p. 56.

St. Andrew's Episcopal Church, 947 Main Street, Barboursville, WV, 25504; (304) 736-1187; The Reverend Edward Mills III; 120 members; town; p. 42.

St. Anne Roman Catholic Church, PO Box 2425, Santa Ana, CA, 92707; (714) 835-7434; Father Joseph Justice; 7000 families; urban; p. 79.

St. Anne Parish, (Roman Catholic); Barrington, IL, 60010; (708) 381-5721; Sister Lorraine Menheer; 7000 parishioners; suburban; p. 21.

St. Gerard Majella Church, (Roman Catholic); 1860 Washington St., Canton, MA, 02021; (617) 828-3219; Father William R. Coen; 600 families; suburban; p. 19.

St. Joseph's Parish, (Roman Catholic); Route 2, Perryville, Apple Creek, MO, 63775; (314) 788-2330; Father John Bolderson; 522 parishioners; rural; p. 25.

St. Jules Catholic Church, 116 St. Jules Street, Lafayette, LA, 70506; (318) 234-2727; Father Wayne Duet; 1000 families; urban; pp. 22, 62.

St. Luke Presbyterian Church, 3121 Groveland School Rd., Wyzata, MN, 55319; (612) 473-7378; Reverend Richard Lundy; 400 members; suburban; p. 22.

Index of Congregations in this book (continued)

Selected Books, Directories, Films, Videos

Your Denomination

Your denomination is an excellent source for outreach/mission materials. Be sure to contact the regional and national offices to find out what they have to offer, including guides, curriculum materials, videos, and descriptions of their programs both in the U.S. and abroad.

Books

Bloom, Dorothy. *Church Doors Open Outward: A Practical Guide to Beginning Community Ministry*. Valley Forge, PA: Judson Press, 1987. Contact: 1-800-458-3766.
> A basic guide with bible study suggestions, group study options, examples of projects.

Bobo, Kim et al. *Organizing for Social Change: A Manual for Activists in the 1990s*. Washington DC: Seven Locks Press, 1991. Contact: 1-800-354-5348.
> Comprehensive guide featuring practical procedures for activists in organizing around issues, building coalitions, fundraising, media relations, etc.

Bos, A. David. *A Practical Guide to Community Ministry*. Louisville KY: Westminster/John Knox Press, 1993. Contact: (502) 569-5043.
> Local community ministry with strong emphasis on ecumenical approaches.

Callahan, Kennon L. *Twelve Keys to an Effective Church*. New York: HarperCollins, 1983. 1-800-331-3761.
> A comprehensive and practical book spanning mission, leadership, decisionmaking, worship.

Campolo, Anthony. *Ideas for Social Action: A Handbook on Mission and Service for Christian Young People*. Grand Rapids, MI: Zondervan Publishing House, 1991 (revised and updated edition). 1-800-727-3480.
> Excellent book for involving young people. Covers service projects, work camps, mission trips, impacting the political system, raising funds for social action, and more. Usefulness not limited to Christians, or to young people for that matter.

Chappell, Tom. *The Soul of a Business: Managing for Profit and the Common Good*. New York: Bantam Books, 1993. Contact: 1-800-223-5780. Not about congregational outreach, but about incorporating the concepts of goodness and the common good in the operation of a private company which, among other things, reaches beyond itself in donating a percentage of its profits to make the world a better place. A most inspiring book by the president of Tom's of Maine (known best for its natural ingredients toothpaste)

Community Family Life Services (CFLS). *Through the Power of the Spirit: A Case Study in the Development and Operation of a Transitional Housing Facility*. Washington, D.C.: CFLS, 1991. (202) 347-0511.
> Just what the title describes: an excellent write-up of how CFLS/Third Trinity Lutheran Church created and operates transitional housing (in the building's basement is the 3rd & Eats restaurant — see p. 57). Includes very useful appendix of contracts, applications and other forms.

Books (continued)

Dudley, Carl S. *Basic Steps Toward Community Ministry.* Washington D.C.: Alban Institute, 1991. (202) 244-7320.
Insights drawn from studies of 38 Illinois and Indiana churches (identified in an appendix) involved in community ministry. Three sections cover: social context, congregational identity, and organizing for social ministry.

Dudley, Carl S. and Douglas A. Walrath. *Developing Your Small Church's Potential.* Valley Forge, PA: Judson Press, 1988. Contact: 1-800-458-3766.
A useful book for small churches wanting to gain strength, bring about change in their communities.

Flanagan, Joan. *The Grass Roots Fundraising Book: How To Raise Money in Your Community.* Chicago: Contemporary Books, Inc., 1992. Contact: (312) 540-4500.
Although not written specifically for churches and synagogues, a useful book with ideas and "how to" information on a wide range of activities, from planning the simplest of special events to holding benefits and raising funds from foundations.

Kroloff, Rabbi Charles A. *54 Ways You Can Help the Homeless.* Southport, CT: Hugh Lauter Levin Associates, Inc. and West Orange, NJ: Behrman House Inc., 1993. Contact: (203) 254-7733.
A wonderful little book offering an understanding of the homeless and specific things to do. Publishers' profits are donated to homeless relief; nonprofits may reproduce the book's contents.

Landsberg, Rabbi Lynne F. and Saperstein, Rabbi David, editors. *Common Road To Justice: A Programming Manual for Blacks and Jews.* Washington D.C: The Marjorie Kovler Institute for Black-Jewish Relations of the Religious Action Center of Reform Judaism, 1991. Contact: (202) 387-2800.
Joint programming manual that summarizes hundreds of joint efforts by black churches and Jewish congregations throughout the country; includes names, telephone numbers. Many program concepts could be used by pairs of congregations of any faith or color.

Mead, Frank S.; revised by Hill, Samuel S. *Handbook of Denominations in the United States.* 9th ed. Nashville TN: Abingdon Press, 1990. Contact: (615) 749-6000.
Includes essentials of the faith and history of each of more than 200 denominations (Christian, Jewish, Buddhist, Muslim and more) found in the U.S. Fascinating and helpful to anyone interested in grasping the enormous diversity, understanding basic similarities and differences.

National Council of Churches of Christ in the U.S.A, Kenneth Bedell, editor. *Yearbook of American & Canadian Churches.* Nashville, TN: Abingdon Press. Annual. Contact: (615) 749-6000.
Comprehensive source of listings (addresses, telephone numbers, officers, brief histories) of religious bodies (state, regional and national offices); also cooperative and ecumenical agencies, seminaries, periodicals, as well as articles and denominational statistics. Includes listings for 35 Jewish organizations.

Pappas, Anthony; Douglas Alan Walrath, General Editor. *Money, Motivation, and Mission in the Small Church.* Valley Forge, PA: Judson Press, 1989. Contact: 1-800-458-3766.
Much more than just fundraising; contains excellent insights into small church culture and how to develop effective low-budget mission projects in that context.

Sample, Tex. *Hard Living People & Mainstream Christians.* Nashville TN: Abingdon Press, 1993.
    Contact: (615) 749-6000.
    Interview-based book about "hard-living" people — alcoholics, addicts, the unemployed and the violent — and how churches can understand and interact with them. Direct quotes, expletives not deleted, give insights about how to minister better to these people.

Shabecoff, Alice. *Rebuilding Our Communities: How Churches Can Provide, Support, and Finance Quality Housing for Low-Income Families.* Monrovia CA: World Vision, 1992. Contact: 1-800-448-6479.
    An extensive resource of housing involvement concepts, examples, and reference materials.

Strobel, Charles F. Room in the Inn: Ways Your Congregation Can Help Homeless People. Nashville TN: Abingdon Press, 1993, Contact: (615) 749-6000.
    Provides an understanding of who the homeless are and what to do about homelessness, including very practical pointers on how to establish and run a shelter. Explains the "Room at the Inn," a growing interfaith program of individual congregations sheltering people in their own facilities.

Sunderland, Ronald H. and Shelp, Earl E. Handle With Care: A Handbook for Care Teams Serving People with AIDS. Nashville TN: Abingdon Press, 1993, Contact: (615) 749-6000.
    A practical guide to organizing a care team, ministering to psychological, social and emotional as well as physical needs of people with AIDS. Includes an illustrated section on assisting people with shaving, bathing, changing bed linens, etc.

Wilson, Marlene. *How to Mobilize Church Volunteers.* Minneapolis: Augsburg, 1983. Contact: (612) 330-3300.
    Excellent guide on the subject; usefulness not limited to Christians. Insights into outreach as well as pointers on working with volunteers.

Fundraising Guides and Directories

The Foundation Center, 79 Fifth Avenue, New York NY 10003-3076. Contact: 1-800-424-9836. Offers: *The Foundation Center's Guide to Proposal Writing* (1993); *The Foundation Directory and Supplement, 15th ed.* which includes information on 6,300 larger foundations and many other directories. Call for their *Catalog* and information about their libraries in various cities.

The Taft Group, Rockville MD, offers a directory listing foundations and others that donate to religious organizations: *Fundraiser's Guide to Religious Philanthropy (1994).* 1-800-877-8238.

Research Grant Guides, Margate FL, offers: *Directory of Building and Equipment Grants; Directory of Operating Grants;* and *Directory of Grants for Organizations Serving People with Disabilities.* Contact: (407) 795-6129.

Films and Videos

EcuFilm, 810 Twelfth Ave So, Nashville TN 37203; Tel. 1-800-251-4091; in Tennessee, call collect 615-242-6277.
    A media distribution service that consolidates the film and video resources maintained by the Christian Church (Disciples of Christ), Lutheran Church in America, Maryknoll Missioners, National Council of Churches, Presbyterian Church (USA), United Church of Christ, and United Methodist Church. A large collection on many topics. Rentals available.

Insights, 11 Beacon Street, Boston MA 02108. (617) 742-3222. Inquire about a companion *Acting on Your Faith: Congregations Making A Difference* video being planned at the time of publication of this book.

Victor N. Claman conceived the book, developed the research methodology, visited congregations, and served as project director and as principal writer, editor and organizer of the book. Trained as a community planner, he researches, writes and publishes energy conservation guides and other public interest materials. He holds bachelor's and master's degrees from Harvard University, has been active in several professional associations, and has served as a director of the City Mission Society of Boston.

Reverend David E. Butler identified and drafted narratives of most of the stories, visited congregations, and assisted in developing and arranging for review of the initial draft of the book. An ordained minister in the United Church of Christ, he is a graduate of Colgate University and of Union Theological Seminary and presently is the minister at Trinity Church in Northboro, Massachusetts. He, too, has served as a director of the City Mission Society of Boston.

Jessica A. Boyatt was responsible for design and production of the book, served as photographer and photo editor, and assisted in editing and organizing. Trained as a professional photographer, she has a bachelor's degree from Brown University and a master's in visual communications from Ohio University. Her work has won several competitions, and she has been awarded a regional National Endowment for the Arts fellowship in photography.

Diane Forman Kent (left) did research for the *Resources* section, transcribed and analyzed interviews, and helped edit stories.

Jessica W. Forbes provided a variety of valuable support throughout the project.

ACKNOWLEDGEMENTS

In addition to the wonderful cooperation of congregations, clergy and staff members we spoke with and visited throughout the country, we gratefully acknowledge the help of the following during the various phases of work on the book:

Research, initial focus, identification of stories: Rev. Catherine Baker, Rev. Rosalind Banbury-Hamm, Rev. Paul Bang-Uk Chun, Rev. Dale Bard, Rev. Paul Bartling, Rev. James Bell, Rev. Judith Bennett, Rabbi Howard Berman, Rev. Hugh B. Berry, Ms. Mary Lee Blanchard, Rev. Gerald Blevins, Rabbi Herman Blumberg, Rev. Irv Bode, Rev. William Brettmann, Bishop Tod Brown, Rev. Dodd Byers, Rev. Robert Carter, Rev. Jon Chapman, Rev. Eric N. Chavis, Dr. James H. Chesnutt, Rev. Kathryn Choy-Wong, Rev. Carlton Christianson, Fr. Edwin Conway, Sr. Cormelita, Rev. Luis Cortes, Fr. William Coyle, Rev. Davida Foy Crabtree, Rev. Marlene Cumins, Rev. Barbara R. Cunningham, Rabbi Randy Czarlinsky, Rev. John R. Deckenback, Rev. William Dittler, Rev. Jerome Divine, Ms. Priscilla Dunwoody, Ms. Cathy Eck, Rev. Paul Eddie, Rev. Marilynn Edwards, Bishop Lowell Erdahl, Rev. Julia Estrella, Dr. W. Lowell Fairley, Dr. Bruce Fisher, Rev. Phylis Fjeld, Bishop Harry Flynn, Ms. Sandra Friedman, Ms. Elaine Fuller, Rev. Ron Gladen, Rev. Mark Goff, Jonathan Goldberg, Rev. Mary Hicks Good, Rev. Roy Godwin, Rev. Arthur Hadley, Ms. Cleone Hagman, Rev. W. James Halfaker, Bishop Richard Hanifer, Rev. Michael Harper, Rev. Dahler Hayes, Rev. Sally Hill, Rev. J. Houston Hodges, Rev. William Hughes, Rev. E. Eugene Hough, Ms. Inez Ireland, Rev. Norman Jackson, Ms. Peg Jacobs, Dr. Samuel A. Jeanes, Rev. Canon Stephen Jecko, Rev. Douglas Johnson, Ms. Nancy Johnson, Rev. David S. King, Rev. James Kurr, Rabbi Vernon Kurtz, Sr. Elain LaCanne, Rabbi Anton Laetner, Ms. Patty Lance, Rabbi Gary Lang, Rev. James Langley, Rev. Ray Legania, Rev. John Lindner, Rev. Natanael Lizaroza, Rev. Clark Lobenstine, Sr. Deborah Lorentz, Rev. Robert Loshuertes, Rev. J. Grant Lowe, Rev. Robert E. Lucas, Rev. Anne Ludlow, Rev. John MacNaughton, Bishop Joseph Madera, Rev. Jose A. Malayang, Rev. Jill Martinez, Rev. James Arlen Mays, Rev. Robinson McAdam, Rev. Ronald McClean, Ms. Judith McDowell, Rev. William McJunken, Rev. Donald McPherson, Rev. David Meekhof, Sr. Amata Miller, Rev. James H. Miller, Rev. Edmund Millet, Rev. Curtis Mitchell, Rev. Douglas Mitchell, Rev. Mary Ann Moller-Gunderson, Rev. William Moore, Rev. Donald Morlan, Ms. Cathleen Morris, Rabbi Herbert Morris, Ms. Patricia Mumford, Ms. Barbara Murphy, Rev. David Myers, Rev. Jane Mykrantz, Ms. Millie Myren, Rev. Robert Navarro, Rev. Arlo Nau, Rev. Hector Navas, Rev. Gustav C. Nelson, Ms. Johnalee Nelson, Msr. James O'Neil, Ms. Jane Odell, Rev. Bonnie Ogee, Rev. William Ohara, Ms. Suzanne Peterson, Rev. Samuel Phillips, Rev. Delton Pickering, Rev. Robert L. Pierce, Rev. Paul Poehlman, Dr. Eunice Blanchard Poethig, Rev. Rosalind Powell, Rev. Robert D. Rasmussen, Dr. Robert Reno, Rabbi Steven Carr Reuben, Rabbi Larry Robbins, Rev. Nancy Roosevelt, Rabbi Gilbert Rosenthal, Rev. JoAnn Ross, Ms. Valerie E. Russell, Rev. B. Sidney Sanders, Rev. J. Robert Sandman, Rev. Marvin E. Sandness, Rev. Edward A. Schroder, Rev. Donald Scott, Rev. Nancy Scott, Rev. Larry Sebold, Rev. Donald J. Sevetson, Rev. John Sharick, Ms. Myrna J. Sheie, Rev. Barbara Sheldon, Rev. Allen Shumway, Rev. Tom Simpson, Ms. Betty Siuba, Mary Elva Smith, Msr. Jaime Soto, Rev. Richard Sparrow, Rabbi Malcolm Spiro, Rev. Robert H. Stoskopf, Derby Swanson, Rev. Jean Ann Swope, Rev. Thomas Tiller, Rev. Bruce Tischler, Rev. Gary D. Torrens, Canon Tim Vann, Rev. Laurean H. Warner, Jr., Rev. Donna Watson, Rev. Edward Weiskotten, Rev. Carol Willard, Ms. Jane Wynne.

Review of initial draft: Hilda Brush, Bronwyn M. Mellquist, Mary Jane Ott, Bob Urquhart, and Joanne Williams of First Baptist Church in Newton, Newton, MA; Rev. Louise Green, Carl Alsen, Maureen Ellenberger, Jan Roller, and Bob Senior of Sudbury Memorial Congregational Church, Sudbury, MA; Roz Allen, Margot Arnold, Barbara Avery, Dorothy and Domenic Cannistraro, Barbara Davis, Muffin Hester and Murray Nicolson of St. Anne's in the Fields, Lincoln MA; Rabbi Herman Blumberg, Katy Goldner and Leslie Rosenblatt of Temple Shir Tikva, Wayland MA; Reverend Ellis Johnson and Carol Beard, Barbara Brewer, C.C. Coggins, Paul Deats, Chet Douglass, Betty Everett, Joanne Humber, Margaret Jernigan, Ellen Johns, Rachelle Ross, Pat Skillman, Doug Spicer, Bob Stewart, and Elinor Yeo of United Parish of Auburndale, MA.

Review of final draft: David Adams, Michael J. Brown, Reverend Robert Brueckner, Ruth Butler, Daniel Claman, Cathy Fallon, Jayne George, Reverend Lyle Hall, Reverend Susan Hansberry, Reverend H. Dahler Hayes, William Holshouser, Peg Jacobs, Daniel Moscato, Sue Mote, Karen Nolan, Dr. Bernard Reisman, Michael Tennis, Rabbi David Whiman, and Reverend Barbara Whittaker-Johns.

PHOTO CREDITS

Photographers

Jessica A. Boyatt: cover (middle, bottom left, bottom right), *In Appreciation* page (top left), pp. 0 (top, bottom), 7, 9 (middle, bottom), 15, 16, 18, 19, 20 (top), 33, 38, 43, 44, 49, 50-51, 55 (top), 69 (top three), 73, 88-89, 91, 99 (bottom), 118 (bottom), 125 (bottom), 127 (bottom right), 129 (top), 132, 135 (bottom right), 139, 151, 153 (top), 157 (top, bottom), 161, 165 (top, bottom), 168 (bottom), 170, 171 (all except Habitat), 191 (top two).

Beth Boylan: cover (middle left), p. 65 (bottom).

Reverend David Butler: *In Appreciation* page (middle right), pp. 5 (bottom), 9 (top), 17, 24, 25, 27 (bottom), 34, 35, 53, 54, 58, 66, 68, 75 (top two), 78 (top), 84 (top), 85 (top), 108 (bottom left), 120 (top), 129 (bottom), 168 (top).

Alan Chapman: p. 23

Victor N. Claman *In Appreciation* page (all except top left and middle right), pp. 2, 5 (top), 12, 20 (bottom), 21 (bottom two), 27 (top), 28, 29, 30, 31, 39, 45, 46 (top), 47, 48, 57, 59, 67 (top), 71, 74, 77, 79 (top), 86 (top), 87 (middle), 92, 93, 94 (top), 95, 99 (top, middle), 101, 102-105, 106 (bottom), 107, 108 (top),109, 110, 113-117, 118 (top), 119, 120 (bottom), 121, 122 (top), 125 (top), 126, 127 (bottom left), 129 (middle), 134, 135 (top), 136 (middle, bottom), 137 (top left), 150, 152, 154, 155, 165 (middle), 167, 168 (middle), 169, 191 (bottom three).

Gregg Hubbard: pp. 0 (middle), 60, 122 (bottom), 133 (top), 140.

Dorothy Mulligan: pp. 37, 64, 111, 141.

Doug Plummer: p. 69 (bottom).

Photos from congregations and organizations

Advent Lutheran Church, Boca Raton, Florida: p. 56 (bottom). **All Saints Episcopal Church**, Pasadena, California: pp. 36, 67 (bottom), 157 (middle). **Bethany Presbyterian Church**, Cleveland, Ohio: p. 46 (bottom). **Bethel AME Church**, Birmingham, Alabama: p. 76. **Brooklyn Ecumenical Cooperatives**, Brooklyn, New York: p. 72. **Catholic Church of St. Ann**, Marrietta, Georgia: p. 40. **Church of the Holy Apostles**, New York, New York: pp. 26, 137 (bottom left). **Community Church of Christ**, Franconia, New Hampshire: cover (bottom middle), pp. 81, 86 (bottom). **Courtesy of Jenny Godwin**, Greensboro, North Carolina: pp. 6, 127 (to right), 159, 160. **First AME Church,** Los Angeles, California: p. 94 (bottom). **First Friends Meeting,** Greensboro, North Carolina: pp. 63, 65 (top), 136 (top), 171 (habitat only). **Holy Spirit Parish**, Fargo, North Dakota: p. 83 **Irvine United Church of Christ**, Irvine, California: p.41 (bottom). **Johnstown Tribune-Democrat**, Johnstown, Pennsylvania: pp. 11, 82. **KAM Isaiah Israel Congregation**, Chicago, Illinois: p. 85 (bottom). **Oreland Presbyterian Church**, Oreland, Pennsylvania: cover (top), p.87 (top, bottom). **Santa Fe Episcopal Church**, San Antonio, Texas: p.78 (middle, bottom). **Second Baptist Church**, Little Rock, Arkansas: p. 75 (bottom). **Southminster Presbyterian Church**, Dayton, Ohio: p. 56 (top), 153 (bottom). **St. Anne's Catholic Church**, Barrington, Illinois: p. 21 (top). **St. Mark's Episcopal Church**, Corpus Christi, Texas: p. 41 (top), 106 (top). **St. Paul's Episcopal Church**, Alexandria, Virginia: p. 55 (middle). **Summit Chapel United Methodist Church**, Johnstown, Pennsylvania: pp. 84 (bottom), 137 (right). **Trinity United Methodist Church, Des Moines**, Iowa: p. 79 (bottom). **Washington Street United Methodist Church**, Charleston, South Carolina: p. 61, 133 (bottom). **White Memorial Presbyterian Church**, Raleigh, North Carolina: p. 3, 70.

Technical Specifications

This book was created in-house. An advanced desktop computer system was used for design and production. All the photographs were scanned into the computer digitally and incorporated along with the text in a digital layout. The offset printer output negatives directly from the digital data on disk. Hardware used included an Apple Macintosh Quadra 950 with 500MB hard drive and 40MB of RAM, a Nikon Coolscan external (35mm film scanner), a UMax UG630 (flatbed scanner for flat art), an Apple Laserwriter Pro 630 (laser print output for proofing), an APS Syquest 88MB external drive (storage), and an APS DAT tape drive (backup).

Software included Quark XPress 3.2 (page layout), Adobe Photoshop 2.5 (imaging and duotones), Aldus Fetch (image database), Adobe Type Manager (font management). Typefaces are Avant Garde and Palatino. The paper is recycled (50%, including at least 10% post-consumer waste).

TO ORDER ADDITIONAL COPIES

You may want to order copies for:

- Outreach or mission committee members
- Other key laypeople
- Staff members
- A relative or friend
- Your former congregation
- Your library
- Wider distribution

Multiple copies are available at a discount.

If you do not find an order form in the book,
please call 1-800-323-6809 to order.

We welcome:

Your comments. We would love to know what you think of this book. Please call or write to us at Insights, 11 Beacon Street, Boston, Massachusetts 02108.

Your stories, other insights. Do you have stories or insights to share that might be included in a future edition? Please let us know at the address above.